Hiking Waterfalls Alabama

Hiking
Waterfalls
Alabama

A Guide to the State's Best Waterfall Hikes

Joe Cuhaj

FALCONGUIDES

GUILFORD, CONNECTICUT

This book is dedicated to all who find wonder in the rainbows of waterfalls.
Never lose the joy.

FALCONGUIDES®

An imprint of The Rowman & Littlefield Publishing Group, Inc.
4501 Forbes Blvd., Ste. 200
Lanham, MD 20706
www.rowman.com
Falcon and FalconGuides are registered trademarks and Make Adventure Your Story is a trademark of The Rowman & Littlefield Publishing Group, Inc.

Distributed by NATIONAL BOOK NETWORK

Photos by Joe Cuhaj unless otherwise noted
Maps by The Rowman & Littlefield Publishing Group, Inc.

British Library Cataloguing in Publication Information available

Library of Congress Control Number: 2021930365

ISBN 978-1-4930-5186-1 (paper: alk. paper)
ISBN 978-1-4930-5187-8 (electronic)

♾™ The paper used in this publication meets the minimum requirements of American National Standard for Information Sciences—Permanence of Paper for Printed Library Materials, ANSI / NISO Z39.48-1992.

The author and The Rowman & Littlefield Publishing Group, Inc. assume no liability for accidents happening to, or injuries sustained by, readers who engage in the activities described in this book.

Contents

The Hikes

Bankhead National Forest and the Sipsey Wilderness

Bankhead National Forest and Sipsey Wilderness Honorable Mentions

North Alabama

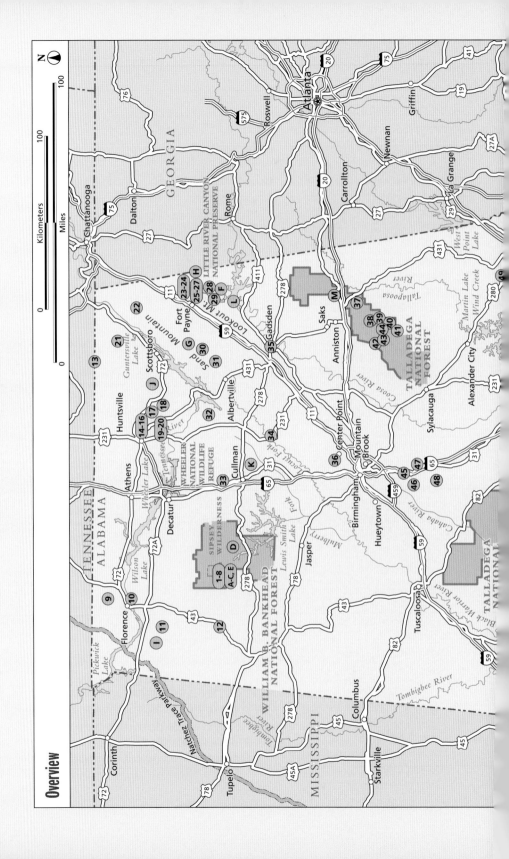

Overview

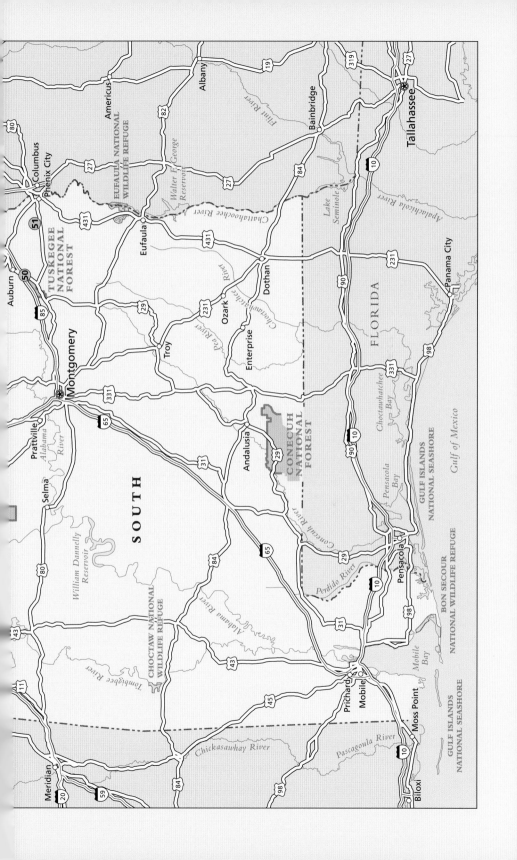

Acknowledgments

As always, a book like this relies on tips and advice from many different people and I can't thank them enough for all the help and patience they gave me, even with my constant barrage of questions. I need to extend a special thanks to some great photographers and people who were kind enough to share their work when my DSLR met with a tragic ending (long story; ask me the next time we meet): Sam Calhoun, Cheaha State Park naturalist Mandy Bear Pearson, Mary Carton, Michael Martin, Eric Wright, David Parham, Melanie Manson and Katey Deasy with the Land Trust of North Alabama, and my good friend Malisa May. Thank you all so much! I also need to thank Talladega National Forest district ranger Gloria Nielsen, DeSoto State Park naturalist Brittany Hughes, and my friend Kim Waites for the advice on some spectacular hidden falls. Yes, Kim, there are some beautiful waterfalls in Alabama that need to be left for people to discover on their own so that they don't become overrun. And thanks to all of you for buying this book. This is my fifth guide for Falcon. The first one, *Hiking Alabama* (now in its 4th edition), was first published twenty years ago in 2000. I wouldn't be here right now if it weren't for you. Thank you.

Introduction

Take a look at the Alabama state seal and what do you see? Miles and miles of rivers and their tributaries veining across the state as they course southward to the Gulf of Mexico. It is estimated that the state has over 132,000 miles of rivers and streams. That doesn't include all its hidden springs and feeder creeks.

What I'm trying to say is, Alabama is one wet state.

The state is as geologically diverse as it is hydrologically with seven general geologic regions. In the southern portion of the state—Mobile and Baldwin Counties—there is the Delta and Coastal region, Alabama's footprint on the Gulf of Mexico, which is flat and where swamps and the second-largest river delta in the country can be found. There are no waterfalls here, but start heading north from this spot and that's where things get interesting for waterfall chasers, and the reason we are here.

The northern and central portions of the state from Birmingham to Huntsville are part of the geologic regions known as the Highland Rim; Cumberland Plateau, Valley, and Ridge; and Piedmont. It's in these regions where those creeks, streams, and

Refreshing—catching some sun and swimming along Cheaha Creek and Devils Den in the Talladega National Forest.

rivers cascade over rocky bluffs and scour out deep canyons and sinkholes to create Alabama's breathtaking natural wonders—its waterfalls.

In these regions, you will find incredible waterfalls around every corner as you hike through what is known as the "Land of a Thousand Waterfalls," the Bankhead National Forest and the Sipsey Wilderness, visit the thundering falls that continue building the deepest canyon east of the Mississippi at Little River, be amazed at the incredible falls that plummet down a 162-foot sinkhole at Neversink Pit, and travel down into the spectacular bowl canyon known as the Walls of Jericho for a beautiful water show. And those are only the highlights.

But Alabama—which is also known by its marketing moniker, the "State of Surprises"—really does surprise you when it comes to waterfalls, because even as far south as Auburn where the terrain is relatively flat, there are a few impressive cascades that we will visit.

My goal for *Hiking Waterfalls Alabama* is to not only present some of the best waterfalls the state has to offer, but also provide treks of varying degrees of difficulty. There are some difficult hikes to waterfalls that lurk deep in Alabama's forests just waiting for you to pay them a visit, as well as easy to moderate hikes for beginning and intermediate skill level hikers. I have included roadside waterfalls where you can simply drive up, step out of your car, and relax to the calming sounds of nature's perfect Zen flow, plus a few trails that are ADA accessible.

I have also included some "honorable mention" hikes. These are waterfalls that didn't make the main list of falls covered in this book for one reason or another, but you should really check them out.

Sadly, there are many more waterfalls that are not covered in this book for one reason or another. For some, I was asked by authorities not to publicize them due to their dangerous nature. Others are very secluded, hidden away with few (if any) visitors, providing incredible solitude for those who find them, and they deserve to remain that way. Many more, however, are now inaccessible, having been purchased and marked "private" by their owners.

All the hikes in this book are day hikes, and while this book isn't a guide to backpacking, I will point out wherever possible how you can make some of these treks into amazing overnight jaunts.

Now, I know that some of you will have questions. The first: Why didn't you include the spillway from such-and-such dam? With only one or two minor exceptions, all waterfalls I have selected are natural falls, and those with dams are usually teamed up with another waterfall, like hike 43, Devils Den and Lake Chinnabee Spillway, where I have tacked on a hike to the lake's dam, built in the 1930s by the Civilian Conservation Corps (CCC), that you can view after visiting the amazing turbulent waters of Devils Den.

In that same vein, the second question will probably be: Why didn't you include this waterfall or that waterfall? Let me tell you, deciding which waterfalls to include was difficult, especially when you're talking about the Bankhead National Forest and the Sipsey Wilderness, where I could write an entire book on that area alone. There are limitations, but I think you will enjoy what I have selected for you with the hopes that they will spark your curiosity to explore and discover even more of Alabama's spectacular waterfalls on your own.

OK, enough of this. Let's lace up our hiking boots and start exploring the waterfalls of Alabama. First, a few definitions I'll be using in the book.

Definitions

Block: A type of waterfall that people who see it describe as being "thunderous." It's a wide flow of water that extends across the width of a river or stream. Visit the roadside Great Falls (hike 51) near Auburn to see what I mean.

Cascade: Considered by many the most beautiful type of falls, the water of a cascade tumbles down a craggy rock face or a series of rock levels. See a perfect example from the bluff high above the gorge of hike 40, Nubbin Creek.

Chute: A pressurized flow of water shooting out of a narrow passage. Check out the lower falls of hike 13, Walls of Jericho, after substantial rain.

Multi-step: Similar to a tiered waterfall (see below) except that each series of drops plummets into a pool before cascading over the edge to another pool. Hike 44, Cheaha Falls, is a good example.

Plunge: A waterfall that drops vertically and loses contact with the rock face. An example would be hike 35, Noccalula Falls.

Punchbowl: Similar to the plunge type, a punchbowl waterfall plunges over a rock ledge into a wide catch pool at the bottom where, at least most of the time, swimming is a joy. An example would be hike #8, Caney Creek Falls.

Rock Shelter: A rock shelter is known by many names—ledge, cave, overhang. Basically it is a rock overhang. We call them rock shelters because many of them in Alabama are deep enough that they were used by Native Americans centuries ago for that very purpose. For us and our visit to the state's waterfalls, it gives us a chance to walk under the overhang and behind the curtain of water of the falls. We will visit many including Caney Creek (hike 8) and Noccalula (hike 35).

Seasonal: A waterfall that is only present during certain times of the year, mainly when there is plentiful rain. These falls are usually nonexistent in the state's hot summers, but can really flow after a good, heavy summer thunderstorm. There are a few examples of these on hike 5, Borden Creek.

Segmented: Several streams of water that run parallel to each other down the same rock ledge. The falls of Bethel Spring (hike 18) is the perfect example with several streams flowing down its rocky face.

Tier: The water from a stream or creek falls over multiple drops. Cheaha Falls (hike 44) is a tiered waterfall.

For Your Safety

There are some inherent safety considerations when hiking waterfalls. These are pretty much no-brainer, commonsense tips, but they need to be said.

First and foremost, watch your step. The area around waterfalls is slippery from the spray and a buildup of moss and algae, not only at the base of the falls but around its headwaters as well, that could cause an unfortunate slip and serious injury. This is especially true at the waterfalls described in this book where you can walk under a rock ledge behind the curtain of water.

You need to also watch your step at the edge of canyons, gorges, and steep trails. Enjoy the view but stay away from the edge. Be especially careful with children and dogs at the edges by keeping them away and close at hand. Dogs should always be kept on a leash for their safety.

For the most part, you will be hiking rock- and boulder-strewn paths to get to a waterfall. Watch where you put your hands and where you sit. Snakes love to hide in the nooks and crannies or sun themselves on the warm rocks.

And then there are ticks. Hopefully, you'll have a group of hikers walking ahead of you to clear the way. Just kidding! The Centers for Disease Control (CDC) suggests using a repellent that contains DEET, while many hikers prefer a spray with permethrin. The best advice is to experiment to find the brand that works for you. In the meantime, keep doing those tick-checks. Every so often while on the trail, check around your ankles. Ticks don't fall out of trees. They start low and head high. Then when you get home, do the full body check.

How to Use This Guide

It goes without saying but I'll say it anyway. To have a safe and memorable hike, you need to plan ahead and be prepared. Within these pages, you will find everything you need to know to have a memorable and safe hike.

First of all, to help you quickly find a hike that is best suited for your interests and abilities, we have included a simple trail finder that breaks hikes out by categories like best swimming, best for children, best fall foliage, and so on.

The hikes I will present are broken down into four regions—Bankhead National Forest and Sipsey Wilderness, and North, Central, and South Alabama—making it easier for you to find a waterfall near whatever part of the state you find yourself in. Each hike begins with a short summary paragraph that gives you a quick idea about the hike and the waterfall itself. The summary is designed so that you can thumb through the book and take a quick glance to see if one piques your interest.

Then we get into the nuts and bolts, the details of the hike and waterfall. The hike details are simple bullet points packed with information about the trek:

- **Height of falls:** Total number of feet from top to base.
- **Type of falls:** Cascade, plunge, etc.
- **Distance:** The total number of miles for the hike from beginning to end (not just one way).
- **Difficulty:** How hard the trek is: easy, moderate, or difficult. The rating is for an average hiker but could be different for your condition or experience, making an easy hike moderately difficult, etc.
- **Hiking time:** The time to complete the hike. This is for an average person who walks 2 to 2.5 miles an hour. The time does not include additional time for you to hang out and take in the beauty of the falls, stops for lunch, or your own physical condition and experience that could slow you down.
- **Start:** Where to start your hike, normally from which side of the place where you park.
- **Trail surface:** What the footing is like along the trail, including creek crossings.
- **Best seasons:** The best time of year to visit the waterfall so you're almost always guaranteed a spectacular show, and the times the trail is open. This doesn't mean that a waterfall is not present other times of the year. See the Weather, Waterfalls, and You section for more information.
- **Canine compatibility:** Whether or not your dog is permitted on the trail and any regulations you need to follow.
- **Fees and permits:** If admission is charged or a permit is required.
- **County:** The county the trail is located in.
- **Land status:** Who owns and manages the property on which the trail is located.

- **Trail contact:** Full information on who to contact for more information about a hike, rules and regulations, camping, etc. This includes the mailing address, phone number, and website.

- **Maps:** Where you can find a particular hike in the map book of all map books, the *DeLorme Alabama Atlas & Gazetteer*, and where additional trail maps can be found.

- **Special considerations:** Things to watch for on the trail. For example, if hunting is allowed in the preserve, if mountain bikes share the trail, drop-offs to watch for, etc.

- **Finding the trailhead:** Mile-by-mile directions to the trailhead from a central starting point complete with GPS coordinates for the trailhead and the waterfall.

Each hike is then accompanied by a full description of what you will experience on the trek—a discussion of the falls, interesting landmarks along the trail, wildflowers and scenery you'll pass along the route, how crowded the trail may or may not be, dangerous areas you need to be on the lookout for. Basically, I try to cover everything you need to know about the trek to ensure you have a safe and fun hike before you head out.

Finally, the hikes include a detailed trail map with important landmarks and features to watch for and, of course, the location of the falls on the route. The maps are augmented with mile-by-mile directions down to the tenth of a mile. The only exceptions are roadside waterfalls, which, obviously, do not need maps or directions.

And as a bonus, scattered throughout these pages you'll find a few "waterfall tidbits" with interesting facts about history, geology, and trivia centered around the waterfall or the area of the state in which it's located.

Weather, Waterfalls, and You

Before we go any further, a little heads-up about Alabama weather and how it affects waterfalls and hiking in the state. Many of the waterfalls in Alabama are seasonal. In the scorching heat of summer, you may be expecting to see a glorious waterfall only to arrive and find a dry rock wall. The summertime heat dries them up. That doesn't mean that seasonal waterfalls never exist in summer. They do pop up when there is a sudden southern thunderstorm, but just as quickly they are gone again.

About that heat. If you do go out in the summer, stay hydrated! The southern heat and humidity often creates heat indexes of over 110°F for days on end. Drink plenty of fluids (drinks with electrolytes help), take frequent breaks in the shade, and wear sunblock and a hat.

Be sure to watch for any sign of life-threatening heat exhaustion or heatstroke: nausea, vomiting, headache, lightheadedness, fainting, weakness, fatigue, confusion, lack of coordination, low blood pressure, or rapid pulse. If you see any of these symptoms:

- Seek shade
- Lie down and elevate the feet and legs

- Apply a wet cloth to the head and neck (other parts of the body if you can)
- Sip cool liquids
- If the victim has a weak pulse, red and hot skin, and shallow breathing, cool them the best way you can and immediately call for emergency aid.

While the hikes described within these pages are located generally in the north and central region far from the Gulf of Mexico, hurricanes and tropical storms can still be dangerous. In fact, more people die from drowning inland far from where a storm makes landfall than where it directly hits. Many of the hikes I cover are in deep gorges and canyons that are prone to flash flooding. If there is a tropical storm or hurricane approaching—or even if severe thunderstorms are in the forecast—pay close attention to alerts and warnings from the National Hurricane Center, National Weather Service, and local media outlets to determine whether or not it is safe to visit that waterfall or if you should make plans to visit another day.

Leave No Trace

You probably know this already, but it never hurts to do a little refresher—when you're out on the trail, please practice these Leave No Trace (LNT) principles to protect our environment and the wildlife that call it home:

- Before heading out, plan your trip and be prepared. This not only includes becoming familiar with the route you will be traveling but also knowing the park's or forest's rules and regulations, what type of weather can be expected, and where you can find help in case of emergencies. And speaking of emergencies, you should never hike alone, and if you do, always let someone know your hike plans—your route and what time you expect to complete your hike.
- Be sure to dispose of waste properly. Remember the rule—pack it in, pack it out. Whatever trash you make on your hike, pack it out with you for proper disposal.
- Of course, when you're on the trail and you gotta go, you gotta go. And despite what some might say, dog droppings are not good fertilizer. For human and dog waste, dig a 6- to 8-inch cat hole well off the trail and away from water sources (about 200 feet) to deposit the waste, then cover the hole. If you're on a short hike with your dog, carry poop bags and pack the waste out.
- Leave what you find! Leave any historic artifacts (arrowheads, Civil War bullets, etc.), antlers, rocks, or wildflowers you may find. Don't deface rocks or plants. Remember, take only pictures, leave only footprints.
- Be respectful of wildlife. Never feed animals and only view them from a distance. If you bring your dog, be sure to keep it under control and avoid encounters.
- Finally, be considerate of others. Be respectful while on the trail—talk quietly, take breaks off the trail, yield to other trail users, and make sure to manage your pet.

For more information and helpful tips, visit LNT online at www.lnt.org.

Trail Finder

Author's Favorite Waterfall Hikes

4. Feather Hawk Falls
7. Mize Mill and Turkey Foot Falls
11. Cane Creek Canyon Nature Preserve
13. Walls of Jericho
17. Lost Sink
18. Bethel Spring
21. Neversink Pit
23. DeSoto Falls
37. Little Hillabee Falls

Least Crowded Waterfall Hikes

1. Auburn Falls
9. Shoal Creek Preserve
17. Lost Sink
20. Talus Falls
21. Neversink Pit
37. Little Hillabee Falls
38. Angel Falls
39. Shinbone Falls
40. Nubbin Creek
41. High Falls
51. Great Falls

Most Crowded Waterfall Hikes

2. Kinlock Falls
3. Parker Falls and Cascade
8. Caney Creek Falls
10. Wilson Dam Waterfall
11. Cane Creek Canyon Nature Preserve
12. Dismals Canyon
13. Walls of Jericho
14. Fagan Springs
16. Lodge and McKay Hollow Falls
19. Alum Hollow
24. DeSoto Falls Picnic Area
28. Little River and Little Falls
30. High Falls Park
36. Turkey Creek Falls
43. Devils Den and Lake Chinnabee Spillway

44. Cheaha Falls
46. Moss Rock Preserve
47. Peavine Falls

Best Secluded Waterfall Hikes

1. Auburn Falls
9. Shoal Creek Preserve
21. Neversink Pit
37. Little Hillabee Falls
40. Nubbin Creek
48. Falling Rock Falls

Best Year-Round Waterfall Hikes

2. Kinlock Falls
8. Caney Creek Falls
10. Wilson Dam Waterfall
22. Pisgah Gorge
23. DeSoto Falls
24. DeSoto Picnic Area
26. Indian Falls
30. High Falls Park
35. Noccalula Falls
36. Turkey Creek Falls
43. Devils Den and Lake Chinnabee Spillway
44. Cheaha Falls
47. Peavine Falls
51. Great Falls

Best Swimming Waterfall Hikes

2. Kinlock Falls
8. Caney Creek Falls
28. Little River and Little Falls (Little Falls only)
33. Hurricane Creek Park
34. Mardis Mill Falls
36. Turkey Creek Falls
43. Devils Den and Lake Chinnabee Spillway
44. Cheaha Falls

Best Waterfall Hikes for Children

5. Borden Creek
6. Fall Creek Falls
10. Wilson Dam Waterfall
12. Dismals Canyon
15. Dry Falls

29. Graces High Falls
42. Hopeful Falls
45. Boulder Canyon
46. Moss Rock Preserve
49. Hidden Falls

Best Roadside Waterfalls

24. DeSoto Falls Picnic Area
28. Little River and Little Falls (Little River Falls boardwalk)
29. Graces High Falls
31. Red Mill (Scarham Creek) Falls
32. Shoal Creek Falls
51. Great Falls

Best ADA-Accessible Waterfall Hikes

10. Wilson Dam Waterfall
22. Pisgah Gorge
24. DeSoto Falls Picnic Area
25. Azalea Cascade, Laurel and Lost Falls Loop (boardwalk to Azalea Cascade only)
28. Little River and Little Falls (Little River boardwalk only)
29. Graces High Falls
30. High Falls Park (rim walk only)
35. Noccalula Falls (upper gorge only)
51. Great Falls (roadside)

Best Hikes to Waterfalls over 50 feet Tall

 4. Feather Hawk Falls
15. Dry Falls
17. Lost Sink
18. Bethel Spring
21. Neversink Pit
22. Pisgah Gorge
23. DeSoto Falls
24. DeSoto Falls Picnic Area
29. Graces High Falls
35. Noccalula Falls
40. Nubbin Creek (Mill Shoal Cascade)
48. Falling Rock Falls

Best Waterfall Hikes with History

12. Dismals Canyon
27. Lodge Falls
50. Natural Falls

MAP LEGEND

Municipal

≡(75)≡ Interstate Highway

≡(421)≡ US Highway

≡(835)≡ State Road

≡(457)≡ County/Forest Road

├──┼──┤ Railroad

···─··─··· State Boundary

Trails

▪▪▪▪▪▪ Featured Trail

▬ ▬ ▬ Trail

Water Features

Lake/Reservoir

River/Creek

Intermittent Stream

Waterfall

Rapid

Spring

Land Management

National Park/Forest/
Recreation Area

National Wilderness

State/Local Park/
Wildlife Area/Preserve

Symbols

∩ Arch/Cave

⇌ Boat Ramp

⊐⊏ Bridge

▲ Campground

⊛ Capital

† Cemetery

•─• Gate

▬ Lodging

🅿 Parking

⊞ Picnic Area

▪ Point of Interest/Structure

📷 Ranger Station

👥 Restrooms

⦀ Stairs

🗼 Tower

○ Town

① Trailhead

🖼 Viewpoint/Overlook

❓ Visitor/Information Center

Bankhead National Forest and the Sipsey Wilderness

L et's jump right in with an amazing region of the state that is known as the "Land of a Thousand Waterfalls"—the Bankhead National Forest and the Sipsey Wilderness. This is an area where, as you hike past tall bluffs and beneath deep rock shelters, it looks like there is a cascade tumbling around every bend. The waterfalls described here are only a small sample of what you will find. As one hiker told me, if you want to find more, just follow your ears.

The forest is located in northwest Alabama in the geologic Cumberland Plateau region. Here, a plateau of sandstone was etched away by the elements and myriad streams, creeks, and rivers, giving way to a limestone, shale, and dolomite base that has

A tiered seasonal cascade reflects the morning sun along the Borden Creek Trail.

been eroded even further over the centuries, leaving behind beautiful canyons that invite exploring. Those streams and rivers continue to remake the face of the forest to this day, giving us the perfect venue to hunt waterfalls.

The Bankhead covers over 180,000 acres of forested land with 90 miles of recreational trails, six recreation areas (some of which offer camping), miles and miles of creeks and streams, and those spectacular waterfalls. Within that acreage, over 25,000 acres were set aside by Congress to protect a fragile landscape where one of the nation's "Wild and Scenic Rivers," the Sipsey Fork, meanders along its channel, continuing to carve out the canyon, making the Sipsey Wilderness a true hiker and backpacker paradise.

The falls listed in this section are only a small sample of the named falls you will find in the Bankhead and Sipsey. This doesn't even begin to include the dozens of unnamed falls that can be found just off the trail or the countless pop-up waterfalls that appear along the trails after rain.

Remember, all trails in a wilderness area and most in our national forests are not blazed. The only thing that identifies them are carved wooden signs at intersections indicating trail names and directions. While most of the trails are well worn and easy to follow, you should have some knowledge of orienteering (using a map and compass). You may encounter dead spots with your GPS, and cell phone service can be spotty if it exists at all.

While trails are not blazed in the Sipsey Wilderness, trail intersections are well marked.

A few of the trails described here can be joined together to make incredible overnight (or longer) backpacking trips. Visit www.sipseywilderness.org for more suggestions and additional maps.

Camping is allowed throughout the national forest and wilderness using what is called the dispersed method of camping. See Appendix A: Camping in the National Forests of Alabama for rules and regulations.

If more modern amenities are to your liking when camping, then the two USDA Forest Service recreation areas are for you. Both the Corinth and Clear Creek Recreation Areas offer improved campsites, playgrounds, clean bathhouses, and swimming in Smith Lake. Visit www.recreation.gov to learn more.

Keep in mind that hunting is allowed throughout the forest. For each hike described, please visit the trail contact's website for specific dates and restrictions during hunting season.

OK, let's visit the Land of a Thousand Waterfalls.

1 Auburn Falls

Meander along the banks of Thompson Creek, past flowering trillium (in season) and the dark and moody green rocks and bluffs of the Sipsey Wilderness with this easy walk to Auburn Falls. Be ready to get your feet a little wet with two creek crossings.

Height of falls: 40 feet
Type of falls: Tiered cascade
Distance: 3.4 miles out and back
Difficulty: Easy
Hiking time: About 1.5 hours
Start: At the Thompson Creek trailhead to the south
Trail surface: Dirt and rock footpath, 2 creek crossings
Best seasons: Sept–June; open sunrise–sunset
Canine compatibility: Dogs permitted; leash required
Fees and permits: None

County: Lawrence
Land status: Wilderness area
Trail contact: Bankhead National Forest, Bankhead Ranger District, 1070 Hwy. 33, Double Springs; (205) 489-5111; www.fs .usda.gov/detail/alabama/about-forest/ districts/?cid=fsbdev3_002553
Maps: *DeLorme: Alabama Atlas & Gazetteer.* Page 23, B9; additional trail maps available online at www.sipseywilderness.org
Special considerations: Hunting is permitted in the wilderness. Contact the Bankhead National Forest for seasons.

Finding the trailhead: From Double Springs, at the intersection of AL 33 and US 278, take US 278 north 0.2 mile and turn right onto AL 195/Haleyville Road. Travel 9.1 miles and turn right onto Kinlock Road. Drive north on Kinlock Road 6.5 miles (after 2.1 miles, the roads from there to the trailhead are dirt and gravel). Turn right onto FS 203 and travel 0.4 mile, then turn right onto FS 208. Follow the dirt road 3.8 miles. The forest service asks that you park just before crossing the bridge so that vehicles can use the wide area on the other side as a turnaround. The actual trailhead is on the other side of the bridge. Trailhead GPS: N34 20.443' / W87 28.220'; Falls GPS: N34 19.542' / W87 27.605'

The Hike

A nice, easy meander along the banks of Thompson Creek gives us the perfect opportunity to get our feet wet—literally and figuratively—when it comes to hiking the Sipsey Wilderness, and visit an often overlooked waterfall in the forest, Auburn Falls.

This waterfall is a 40-foot, three-tier cascade that flows down a sheer rock wall just off Trail 206, the Thompson Creek Trail. In the right light, the falls produces beautiful colors as the moss surrounding the tiers lights up with vibrant greens and the rocks take on a bluish sheen from the spray. Auburn Falls is beautiful but seasonal and may not be running in late summer.

The trail itself, Trail 206, is an easy walker that follows the banks of its namesake creek. The trail is brightened in season with purple trillium, yellow violets, and red

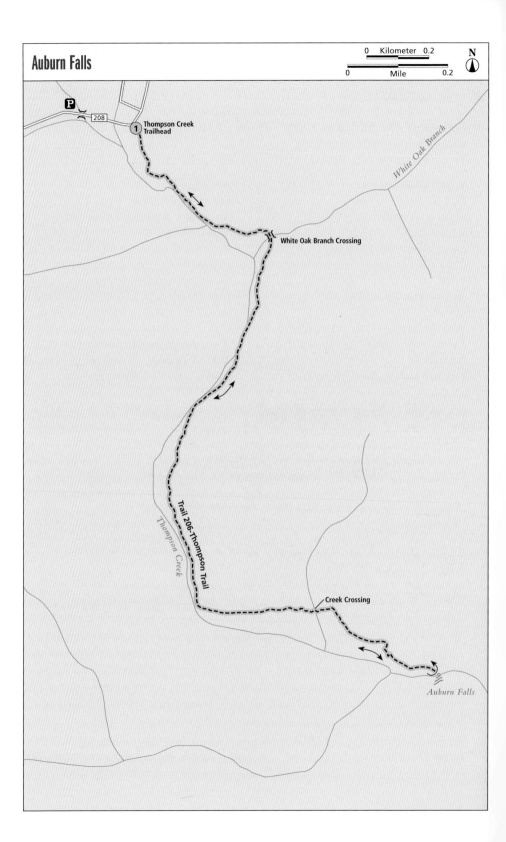

Auburn Falls

0   Kilometer   0.2

0   Mile   0.2

N

P

208

Thompson Creek
Trailhead

1

White Oak Branch

White Oak Branch Crossing

Trail 206-Thompson Trail

Thompson Creek

Creek Crossing

Auburn Falls

Follow the banks of Thompson Creek to visit our first stop in the Sipsey Wilderness—Auburn Falls.
PHOTO COURTESY SAM CALHOU

buckeye. Thompson Creek puts on a show itself when the water is just right, with fast and frothy shoals racing through its boulder-strewn channel.

As with all trails in the wilderness, it is not blazed, but it's easy enough to follow the well-worn path. You will have to make two creek crossings, one across White Oak Branch, which feeds Thompson Creek at mile 0.4, the other an unnamed branch at mile 1.4. The crossings aren't usually too bad and fairly shallow, but that, of course, is all dependent on recent rains.

While we describe only the trip to the falls here, you can continue south on Trail 206 another 0.8 mile to scramble up Ship Rock, a gigantic boulder that looks, well, like a ship.

If you wish to spend the night, you can do so at any of the established campsites near the creek. See Appendix A: Camping in the National Forests of Alabama for information.

Miles and Directions

0.0 Begin by heading south from the Thompson Creek trailhead on FS 208.

0.4 Cross White Oak Branch and continue south on Trail 206.

1.4 Cross an unnamed creek to the east.

1.7 Arrive at Auburn Falls. When ready, turn around and return to the trailhead.

3.4 Arrive back at the trailhead.

2 Kinlock Falls

Kinlock Road can be considered one of the Bankhead's waterfall corridors. Within 0.7 mile you will find two incredible cascade waterfalls. One we'll visit in our next hike, but first we'll stop at this popular swimming hole—Kinlock Falls, a 25-foot-wide, 15-foot-tall cascade that churns white down into a deep, cold pool. It's a definite must-see when you're in the forest.

Height of falls: 15 feet, 25 feet wide
Type of falls: Cascade
Distance: 0.3 mile out and back
Difficulty: Easy to view from a bluff, moderate to base
Hiking time: About 30 minutes
Start: From the narrow pull-off on the north side of Kinlock Road
Trail surface: Rock, gravel
Best seasons: Year-round; open sunrise–sunset
Canine compatibility: Dogs permitted; leash required
Fees and permits: None

County: Lawrence
Land status: Wilderness area
Trail contact: Bankhead National Forest, Bankhead Ranger District, 1070 Hwy. 33, Double Springs; (205) 489-5111; www.fs .usda.gov/detail/alabama/about-forest/ districts/?cid=fsbdev3_002553
Maps: *DeLorme: Alabama Atlas & Gazetteer:* Page 23, B9; additional trail maps available online at www.sipseywilderness.org
Special considerations: Bring a bag along to pick up any trash you find and help keep the falls clean.

Finding the trailhead: From Double Springs, at the intersection of AL 33 and US 278, take US 278 north 0.2 mile and turn right onto AL 195/Haleyville Road. Travel 9.1 miles and turn right onto Kinlock Road. Drive 3.6 miles and park in the narrow shoulder on either side of the highway (if you crossed the bridge over Hubbard Creek, you passed the parking area). Be sure to pull far enough off the roadway. There is room for 3, maybe 4, cars. The trail begins on the north side of the road. Trailhead GPS: N34 18.455' / W87 30.192'; Falls GPS: N34 18.514' / W87 30.155'

The Hike

Kinlock Falls is part of a designated historic district within the Bankhead National Forest that has seen human habitation for centuries. Included in this area is the famous Kinlock Falls, a popular swimming hole for locals and visitors to the Bankhead National Forest for as long as anyone can remember.

The falls itself can be found just off Kinlock Road by taking this short 0.3-mile out-and-back hike. This is an unofficial path, although it has been used so much over the years that I guess you could call it "official." The trail is an un-blazed rock and gravel path that begins on the north side of Kinlock Road from where you park. Climb down a short set of stairs from the road, and in less than 0.1 mile, you will get your first look at the falls from a bluff.

Kinlock Falls, Parker Falls and Cascade

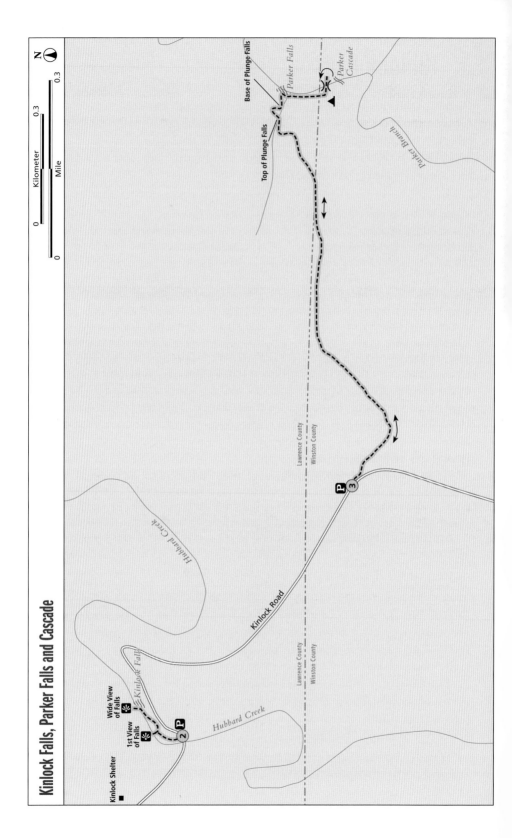

You won't find a much better swimming hole than the one at the base of Kinlock Falls.

From here it's basically pick your way down to the base of the falls, but use extreme caution on the steep, rocky descent. In less than 0.2 mile, you will arrive at the base of the falls. The water is cold and inviting on a hot summer day. I haven't taken a dip in the pool myself, but I can see that climbing out up the steep, rocky banks near the falls may be a challenge, so you may have to walk down the creek a little bit to get to an easy spot to clamber out. And obviously, there are no lifeguards here so swim at your own risk.

After viewing, simply turn around and retrace your steps to the trailhead.

Only 0.5 mile north of Kinlock Falls is an incredible geologic site, the mammoth rock shelter known as Kinlock Shelter. The shelter was carved into the sandstone rock wall over the centuries by the weathering action of the elements and streams and has seen human activity for thousands of years. Evidence of that history can be seen etched in the rock walls, ancient petroglyphs depicting turkey tracks and straight cuts in the wall where tools were sharpened. It is truly a sight to behold, but remember, this is a protected historic site. Do not take any artifacts you may find. It was also a place of Native American spiritual worship, so treat the site with reverence and dignity. There isn't a trail to the shelter but it's easy to find. From the Kinlock Falls parking area, drive north on Kinlock Road 0.6 mile and park in the large gravel lot on the left. Walk up Kinlock Road a few yards and turn left onto a gated forest service road for 0.2 mile, then turn right (north) into the woods on a faint, nondescript trail to head very steeply downhill. The shelter is at the bottom of the hill. The entire hike is 1 mile out and back. The shelter is located at N34 18.798' / W87 30.525'. Shelter coordinates: N34 18.874' / W87 30.764'.

3 Parker Falls and Cascade

An incredible pair of waterfalls line up along Parker Branch in the Sipsey Wilderness—and all within this 1.8-mile out-and-back hike—the ribbon of water known as Parker Falls, which rushes off a tall rock shelter, and the wide Parker Cascade, which tumbles down into a mossy green bowl canyon.

See map on page 8.
Height of falls: Parker Falls, 40 feet; Parker Cascade, 20 feet
Type of falls: Plunge, tiered, and cascade
Distance: 1.8 miles out and back
Difficulty: Easy to top of first falls, difficult down to the branch
Hiking time: About 2.5 hours
Start: On the east side of Kinlock Road from the parking area
Trail surface: Dirt, rock
Best seasons: Sept–July; open sunrise–sunset
Canine compatibility: Dogs permitted (see Special considerations); leash required
Fees and permits: None

County: Lawrence, Winston
Land status: Wilderness area
Trail contact: Bankhead National Forest, Bankhead Ranger District, 1070 Hwy. 33, Double Springs; (205) 489-5111; www.fs .usda.gov/detail/alabama/about-forest/ districts/?cid=fsbdev3_002553
Maps: *DeLorme: Alabama Atlas & Gazetteer.* Page 23, B9; additional trail maps available online at www.sipseywilderness.org
Special considerations: There are very narrow paths with some precarious drop-offs and a steep climb down into the gorge. Use caution. May not be suitable for children or dogs.

Finding the trailhead: From Double Springs, at the intersection of AL 33 and US 278, take US 278 north 0.2 mile and turn right onto AL 195/Haleyville Road. Travel 9.1 miles and turn right onto Kinlock Road. Drive 2.9 miles and park in the narrow shoulder on either side of the highway (if you crossed the bridge over Hubbard Creek, you passed the parking area). Be sure to pull far enough off the roadway. There is room for 3, maybe 4, cars. The trail begins on the east side of the road. Trailhead GPS: N34 18.199' / W87 29.746'; Falls GPS: Parker Falls, N34 18.308' / W87 29.084'; Parker Cascade, N34 18.245' / W87 29.042'

The Hike

Only a short 1-mile drive south of Kinlock Falls (hike 2) is this wonderful pair of waterfalls all lined up and waiting for you along Parker Branch. This hike gives you a little of everything—a towering 40-foot plunge waterfall called Parker Falls and the spectacular cascade known as, coincidentally enough, Parker Cascade.

The path begins where the pavement ends on Kinlock Road. Park alongside the road and walk the wide gravel opening to the north. In only a few yards, it narrows to a 2-foot-wide, brushy dirt footpath through a hardwood and pine forest. As with other trails in the forest, this one has no blazes. In fact, it is an unofficial trail, but it is used enough that it is easy to follow.

First stop along Parker Branch is the plunge waterfall known as Parker Falls.

Don't be fooled by the ease of the walk when you start this hike. The first 0.7 mile is over fairly level ground, but at the top of Parker Falls, things change drastically. After crossing the top of the falls, you will follow the rim of the gorge for almost 0.2 mile along a very narrow dirt and rock footpath with precipitous drop-offs next to the trail. The trail eventually follows the base of a bluff line very steeply downhill until it reaches the bottom of the gorge and the base of Parker Falls. The falls can slow to just a trickle in late summer during times of dry weather.

You'll want to hang out and relax a bit at the falls, taking in the soothing sounds and glimmering water before you begin heading downstream to your next destination. The route is now an extremely rocky, boulder-strewn path alongside the stream, so much so that you may find yourself crisscrossing the stream several times to make it easier. The stream is fairly shallow most of the time, and I found myself walking the creek instead.

You will pass a nice tiered cascade along the way at mile 0.9 that tumbles over the rocky branch until you finally arrive at Parker Cascade.

Miles and Directions

0.0   Start down a wide gravel area on the east side of the road. In a few yards it becomes a narrow dirt footpath.

0.7   Start hearing Parker Falls and begin an easy descent as the trail becomes rockier. In less than 0.1 mile, arrive at the top of the falls. Cross the top of the falls, then turn right and follow the edge of the gorge. The path is very narrow with a sharp drop-off to the right.

0.8   Begin a *very* steep downhill next to the bluff. In less than 0.1 mile, arrive at the base of Parker Falls.

0.9   Pass a nice tiered cascade. Cross the creek and continue following it to the south. In less than 0.1 mile, pass an established campsite and arrive at Parker Cascade. When ready, turn around and retrace your steps to the trailhead.

1.8   Arrive back at the trailhead.

4 Feather Hawk Falls

Feather Hawk Creek forms a stunning 70-foot plunge down a towering sandstone cove that eventually feeds the Sipsey Fork. Once again, the green moss of the dark canyon brightens the cove as the plunge crashes down onto its boulder-strewn base.

Height of falls: 70 feet
Type of falls: Plunge
Distance: 6.4 miles out and back
Difficulty: Easy with moderate climb down to the Sipsey Fork and up Feather Hawk Creek
Hiking time: About 4 hours
Start: On the north side of the Randolph Trail trailhead
Trail surface: Dirt, gravel, rock
Best seasons: Year-round; open sunrise–sunset
Canine compatibility: Dogs permitted; leash required

Fees and permits: None
County: Winston
Land status: Wilderness area
Trail contact: Bankhead National Forest, Bankhead Ranger District, 1070 Hwy. 33, Double Springs; (205) 489-5111; www.fs .usda.gov/detail/alabama/about-forest/ districts/?cid=fsbdev3_002553
Maps: *DeLorme: Alabama Atlas & Gazetteer.* Page 23, B9; additional trail maps available online at www.sipseywilderness.org
Special considerations: None. Just have fun.

Finding the trailhead: From Double Springs, at the intersection of US 278 and AL 33, take US 278 north 0.2 mile and turn right onto AL 195/Haleyville Road. Travel 9.1 miles and turn right onto Kinlock Road. Drive 1.1 miles and turn right onto Cranal Road/CR 60. Travel 1.5 miles and the Randolph Trail trailhead will be on the left. There is plenty of room for 15 cars. The trail begins on the north side of the parking lot. Trailhead GPS: N34 17.279' / W87 28.283'; Falls GPS: N34 18.522' / W87 26.492'

The Hike

An incredible plunge waterfall just off the Sipsey Fork is easily accessible along the Sipsey Wilderness's Trail 202 (Randolph Trail) and a little walk upstream of the river and up the channel of Feather Hawk Creek.

The hike begins on the north side of the parking lot using both Trail 201 and Trail 202. The trail is basically an old gravel forest service/logging road for about 2.5 miles. It can be a bit overgrown at times but is easy to follow. The path follows along the top of a ridgeline, and while it isn't always a very scenic route to the rim of the canyon, what it lacks in landscapes is more than made up for with wildlife and wildflowers.

Around any bend you may kick up a white-tailed deer or a wild turkey, or spot a fox darting across the path. Birders will recognize Acadian flycatchers, eastern phoebes, and belted kingfishers darting in and out of the brush.

The path is lined with holly, magnolia, and hemlock, and you will be sharing the trail with photographers and wildflower lovers in season as they take to the trail to catch blooming yellow lady slippers, shooting stars, and yellow and white trillium.

Feather Hawk Falls plunges down its sandstone walls, crashing onto its boulder-strewn base.
PHOTO COURTESY SAM CALHOUN

The trail finally leaves the road at mile 2.6 and starts its steepest descent down into the canyon—a 300-foot drop in 0.3 mile down the sandstone wall of the canyon until it bottoms out along the banks of the Sipsey Fork.

Heading upstream a short distance will lead you to Feather Hawk Creek on the left. Just follow the creek bed uphill to arrive at the falls.

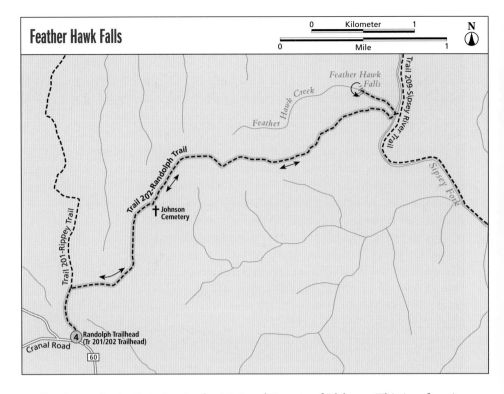

See Appendix A: Camping in the National Forests of Alabama. This is a favorite destination for an overnight, with camping near the river.

Miles and Directions

0.0   The trail begins on the north side of the Randolph Trail trailhead at the information sign on the joint Trail 201 (Rippey Trail) and Trail 202 (Randolph Trail). A wooden sign next to the trail reads "201/202."

0.1   Turn right (southwest) on an old gravel road.

0.2   Come to a Y intersection. Take the right fork (north) to continue on Trail 202 (Trail 201 branches off on the left fork).

1.2   Pass the old Johnson Cemetery.

2.6   Begin steepest descent into the canyon.

2.9   Arrive at the banks of the Sipsey Fork. Turn left (north) and head upstream.

3.0   Come to Feather Hawk Creek on the left. Head up the creek to the northwest.

3.2   Arrive at Feather Hawk Falls. When ready, retrace your steps to the trailhead.

6.4   Arrive back at the trailhead.

Option: For a long 11.3-mile day trip or a great overnight backpacking trek in the Sipsey Wilderness, use this hike along with Trail 209 (Sipsey River Trail) and Trail 204A (East Bee Branch Trail) to visit not only Feather Hawk Falls but also the impressive 70-foot Bee Branch Falls. See Bankhead Forest and Sipsey Wilderness Honorable Mentions for details.

5 Borden Creek

A fun hike for the entire family and a good introduction to hiking in the Sipsey Wilderness is the easy-walking Borden Creek Trail. This hike will take you past several seasonal waterfalls spilling down the sandstone bluffs that line the trail on one side, with the clear, cool waters of the Sipsey Fork and Borden Creek on the other. The hike is highlighted with a little "caving"—a short walk through a 100-foot L-shaped tunnel in the rocks known as Fat Man's Squeeze.

Height of falls: Various, tallest 30 feet
Type of falls: Small plunge and cascade
Distance: 4.4 miles out and back
Difficulty: Easy
Hiking time: About 2 hours
Start: At the Trail 209 (Sipsey River Trail) trailhead on the north side of the Sipsey Wilderness Recreation Area parking lot (under the Cranal Road/CR 60 overpass)
Trail surface: Sand, dirt, rock
Best seasons: Sept–May; open sunrise–sunset
Canine compatibility: Dogs permitted; leash required
Fees and permits: Day-use fee (pay at the kiosk)

County: Winston
Land status: Wilderness area
Trail contact: Bankhead National Forest, Bankhead Ranger District, 1070 Hwy. 33, Double Springs; (205) 489-5111; www.fs.usda.gov/detail/alabama/about-forest/districts/?cid=fsbdev3_002553
Maps: *DeLorme: Alabama Atlas & Gazetteer:* Page 23, C9; additional maps available at www.sipseywilderness.org
Special considerations: Borden Creek and the Sipsey River may flood after heavy rains. Use caution during those times.

Finding the trailhead: From Double Springs, at the intersection of US 278 and AL 33, take AL 33 north 12.6 miles and turn left onto CR 6/Cranal Road. In 2.5 miles, CR 6 becomes CR 60. Continue an additional 1.4 miles and turn left into the Sipsey Wilderness Recreation Area. There is plenty of room for 30 cars. There is also a restroom and a great place where you can picnic and swim in the river. Pay your day-use fee at the unattended fee box. Trailhead GPS for out-and-back hike: N34 17.133' / W87 23.919'; Shuttle trailhead GPS for point-to-point hike: N34 18.567' / W87 23.658'; Falls GPS: Scattered along the trail

The Hike

The Borden Creek hike is an easy walker over a fairly level dirt and rock footpath that ranges in width from 2 to 5 feet wide. There are a few small rock scrambles to navigate but nothing too challenging. But remember, the waterfalls along this trek are seasonal. After a good rain, you will be treated to several cascading down the tall bluffs.

One highlight of the trip is a little adventure that kids of all ages will love—a walk through a small cave called the Fat Man's Squeeze. The cave is only 100 feet long and makes a sharp turn in the middle, making it extremely dark inside. It is a

One of several seasonal waterfalls along Trail 200, the Borden Creek Trail.

very damp cave with a 30-foot seasonal waterfall at the wide northern entrance. The south entrance is narrow. If you are claustrophobic, this isn't for you. Since this is the turnaround for the hike described here, if you don't want to go through the cave, you can wait at the entrance while the rest of your party takes a peek.

Keep in mind that the uniqueness of this trail with its waterfalls and cave plus its relative ease to hike makes it a popular path. On any given weekend the trailhead is full. But don't let that deter you. Just get an early start.

The hike uses two trails—Trail 209 (the Sipsey River Trail) and Trail 200 (the Borden Creek Trail). As mentioned previously, all trails in a wilderness area like the

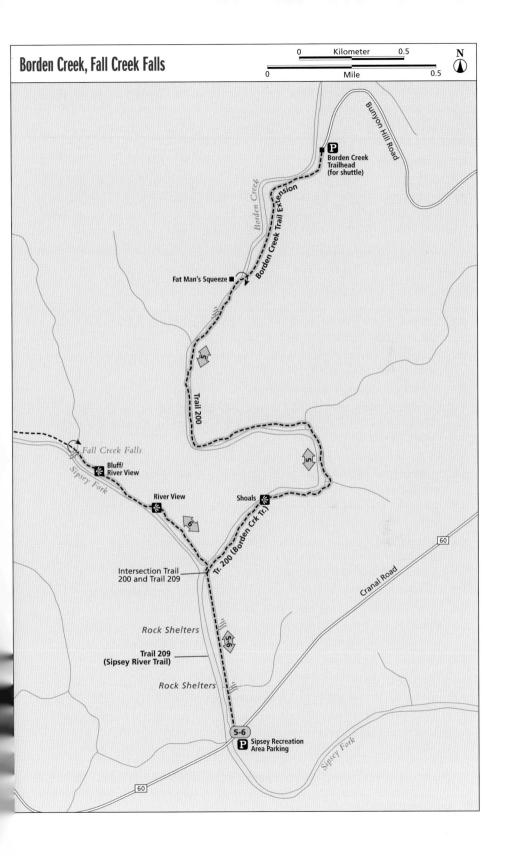

Borden Creek, Fall Creek Falls

Kilometer
0   0.5

Mile
0   0.5

N

Bunyon Hill Road

P Borden Creek Trailhead (for shuttle)

Borden Creek

Borden Creek Trail Extension

Fat Man's Squeeze ■

5

Trail 200

5

Fall Creek Falls

Bluff/ River View

River View

Shoals

Sipsey Fork

6

5

Tr. 200 (Borden Crk Tr.)

60

Intersection Trail 200 and Trail 209

Cranal Road

Rock Shelters

5-6

Trail 209 (Sipsey River Trail)

Rock Shelters

5-6

P Sipsey Recreation Area Parking

Sipsey Fork

60

Sipsey are not blazed. The only thing that identifies them are carved wooden signs at intersections indicating trail names and directions, but the path is well worn so you shouldn't have trouble finding your way. Having said that, however, there are plenty of game trails and, unfortunately, social trails cut by careless individuals that can lead you off track. Always carry a GPS to help you navigate, and study up on basic orienteering skills (using a map and compass), but don't forget to carry that map and compass with you.

You can do this hike as a 4.4-mile out-and-back (as described in the Miles and Directions), or you can do a 2.8-mile point-to-point that would require a shuttle vehicle parked at the Borden Creek trailhead (see Finding the trailhead for coordinates).

You will notice several established campsites along the trail. If you would like to spend a night next to the soothing sounds of Borden Creek, feel free to do so, but use these established sites and do not create new ones.

Miles and Directions

0.0   Start from the north side of the parking lot at the kiosk and pick up Trail 209 (the Sipsey River Trail) under the CR 60/Cranal Road overpass.

0.2   Pass a large bluff with a rock shelter on the right. In 100 feet pass another huge rock overhang with a seasonal waterfall.

0.4   Pass another seasonal waterfall on the right.

0.6   Come to the intersection of Trail 209 and Trail 200 (Borden Creek Trail) at the confluence of Borden Creek and Sipsey Fork. Continue straight (northeast) on Trail 200, following the banks of Borden Creek.

0.9   Cross a rocky creek.

1.0   Pass a shoal in the creek to your left. In 200 feet pass a campsite on the left. There is a nice bluff with shelters on the right.

1.1   Come to a Y intersection. Take the left fork. There is another campsite here. Cross a creek to the northwest and in 100 feet cross a second creek.

1.3   The trail comes to another nice creek. Hike straight across it and pick up the trail on the other side, where you will cross an unmarked trail that heads left and right (north and south). Continue straight to the west.

1.4   The trail moves away from the bluffs and the forest opens up for a short distance.

2.0   Cross an intermittent stream with a small falls here during times of rain.

2.2   Arrive at Fat Man's Squeeze. Walk through the cave; on the other side there is a small, seasonal waterfall. When ready, turn around and head to the trailhead.

4.4   Arrive back at the trailhead.

Option: At mile 2.2 and the Fat Man's Squeeze, you can continue north on the Borden Creek Trail to the Borden Creek trailhead, making this a 2.8-mile point-to-point hike. Just remember that you will need to park a shuttle vehicle at this trailhead so you can get back to the Sipsey Recreation Area.

6 Fall Creek Falls

A truly fun hike is in store for kids of all ages on this easy 2.2-mile out-and-back to Fall Creek Falls. The hike is highlighted with beautiful views of the Sipsey Fork and its shoals plus a fording of the cool, clear waters of Borden Creek where it converges with the Sipsey Fork, a refreshing spot in the summertime. Then there is the center-piece of this hike—Fall Creek Falls—which tumbles down a 25-foot-tall rocky face to a crashing halt on the boulders below.

See map on page 17.
Height of falls: 25 feet
Type of falls: Plunge
Distance: 2.2 miles out and back with 1 stream crossing
Difficulty: Easy
Hiking time: About 1 hour
Start: At the Trail 209 (Sipsey River Trail) trailhead on the north side of the Sipsey Wilderness Recreation Area parking lot (under the Cranal Road/CR 60 overpass)
Trail surface: Sand, dirt, and rock footpaths with a crossing of the sandy-bottomed Borden Creek
Best seasons: Sept–June; open sunrise–sunset
Canine compatibility: Dogs permitted; leash required

Fees and permits: Day-use fee (pay at the kiosk); open sunrise to sunset
County: Winston
Land status: Wilderness area
Trail contact: Bankhead National Forest, Bankhead Ranger District, 1070 Hwy. 33, Double Springs; (205) 489-5111; www.fs .usda.gov/detail/alabama/about-forest/ districts/?cid=fsbdev3_002553
Maps: *DeLorme: Alabama Atlas & Gazetteer*. Page 23, C9; additional trail maps available online at www.sipseywilderness.org
Special considerations: Borden Creek and the Sipsey River may flood after heavy rains. Use caution during those times.

Finding the trailhead: From Double Springs, at the intersection of US 278 and AL 33, take AL 33 north 12.6 miles and turn left onto CR 6/Cranal Road. In 2.5 miles, CR 6 becomes CR 60. Continue an additional 1.4 miles and turn left into the Sipsey Wilderness Recreation Area. There is plenty of room for 30 cars. There is also a restroom and a great place where you can picnic and swim in the river. Pay your day-use fee at the unattended fee box. Trailhead GPS: N34 17.133' / W87 23.919'; Falls GPS: N34 17.837' / W87 24.405'

The Hike

As with all trails in the nation's wilderness areas, the path to Fall Creek Falls is not blazed, but the well-worn path is easy to follow. Intersections are well marked with wooden signs indicating trail names and directions.

Begin on the north side of the parking lot at the Trail 209/200 kiosk. The trail heads north from here as it crosses under the CR 6/Cranal Road overpass.

The path is a nice, level, sand and dirt footpath with a few rocks that follows the banks of the Sipsey Fork until it meets up with Trail 200 (Borden Creek Trail, hike 5)

at the confluence of Borden Creek and Sipsey Fork. Here's where things get interesting, and you'll be getting your feet wet as you turn left and cross Borden Creek to the north. On the other side, there is a short series of steps you will use to scramble up the dirt bank. At the top, turn left to continue on Trail 209.

The path now meanders above the river with good views of the fast shoals and bluffs of the Sipsey Fork to your left until it finally arrives at the falls. Trail 209 continues on from here, but this is our destination and the turnaround for this hike.

Enjoy the water show and, when ready, turn around and retrace your steps to the trailhead. Just remember that after you cross Borden Creek again, turn to the right (south) to head back to the trailhead.

Miles and Directions

0.0 Start from the north side of the parking lot at the kiosk and pick up Trail 209 (the Sipsey River Trail) under the CR 60/Cranal Road overpass.

0.2 Pass a large bluff with a rock shelter on the right. In 100 feet pass another huge rock overhang with a seasonal waterfall.

0.4 Pass another seasonal waterfall on the right.

0.6 Come to the intersection of Trail 209 and Trail 200 (Borden Creek Trail). Turn left (north) and cross Borden Creek. On the other side, turn left (northwest) to continue on Trail 209.

0.8 Start seeing nice views of the Sipsey Fork below to the left.

0.9 Cross a spring.

1.0 Nice view of the shoals and bluffs of the Sipsey Fork.

1.1 Arrive at the falls. When ready, turn around and begin retracing your steps back the way you came.

1.6 Back at Borden Creek, cross the creek again, this time to the south. On the other side, turn right (south) to continue on Trail 209.

2.2 Arrive back at the trailhead.

Fall Creek Falls showers its rocky base.

7 Mize Mill and Turkey Foot Falls

Only 0.5 mile west of the Sipsey Wilderness Recreation Area, there is a pair of water-falls that you just have to visit when in the wilderness—Turkey Foot Falls and Mize Mill Falls. While the climb down into the canyon is a bit difficult, it is well worth the effort, especially to view Mize Mill, where the sound of the falls surrounds you as it echoes off the sandstone canyon walls.

Height of falls: Turkey Foot Falls, 20 feet; Mize Mill Falls, 20 feet
Type of falls: Turkey Foot, plunge; Mize Mill, cascade
Distance: 0.8 mile out and back
Difficulty: Moderate with a difficult 50-foot vertical climb
Hiking time: About 1 hour
Start: Across from the narrow gravel parking area along CR 60/Cranal Road
Trail surface: Dirt, rock, gravel with stream crossing
Best seasons: Sept–June; open sunrise–sunset
Canine compatibility: Dogs permitted (climb down may be too steep for them; use your best judgment); leash required

Fees and permits: None
County: Winston
Land status: Wilderness area
Trail contact: Bankhead National Forest, Bankhead Ranger District, 1070 Hwy. 33, Double Springs; (205) 489-5111; www.fs.usda.gov/detail/alabama/about-forest/districts/?cid=fsbdev3_002553
Maps: *DeLorme: Alabama Atlas & Gazetteer:* Page 22, B9; additional trail maps available online at www.sipseywilderness.org
Special considerations: There is a steep 50-foot climb down to the bottom of the canyon.

Finding the trailhead: From Double Springs, at the intersection of Adkins Road and AL 195/Haleyville Road, take AL 195 north 1 mile. The road bends to the right and becomes AL 33. Travel 12.6 miles on AL 33 and turn left onto CR 6/Cranal Road. Drive 2.2 miles and CR 6 becomes CR 60/Cranal Road. Drive an additional 2.3 miles. The narrow gravel parking area will be on the left at an old gravel forest service road. The pull-off has room for about 3 cars parked parallel to the road. Don't block the forest service road. The trail begins directly across the road to the north. Trailhead GPS: N34 16.934' / W87 24.406'; Turkey Foot Falls GPS: N34 17.099' / W87 24.347'; Mize Mill Falls GPS: N34 16.989' / W87 24.407'

The Hike

If you haven't noticed by now, Cranal Road, which runs through the Sipsey Wilder-ness, is a waterfall corridor. Let's add another one to the list, the double falls hike to the beautiful Turkey Foot Falls and Mize Mill Falls.

Turkey Foot Falls is a beautiful 20-foot plunge falls that tumbles down the sand-stone cliff into a small catch pool at the bottom. But wait, there's more. Head down the rocky banks of Turkey Creek only 0.2 mile and arrive at the roaring, frothing

The sound of Mize Mill Falls surrounds you as it echoes off the walls of the bowl canyon.

(when it's running full) Mize Mill Falls. The cascade surges down the steps of its sandstone base, the sound surrounding you as it bounces off the narrow canyon walls.

The hike down into the canyon starts off easy enough on a narrow dirt and rock path, taking you to two rocky bluffs for views of Mize Mill Falls. Don't climb down here. Continue down the trail. Hepatica and hemlock brighten the path in season.

Soon you will come to a notch in the rocks and a steep, almost vertical, climb down to the bottom of the canyon. I've seen people bring their dogs and small children down the climb, but it could be tricky and dangerous. Use your best judgment and be safe.

When you arrive at Mize Mill, you'll notice that there are two established campsites with fire rings. Camping is allowed (find out more in Appendix A: Camping in the National Forests of Alabama).

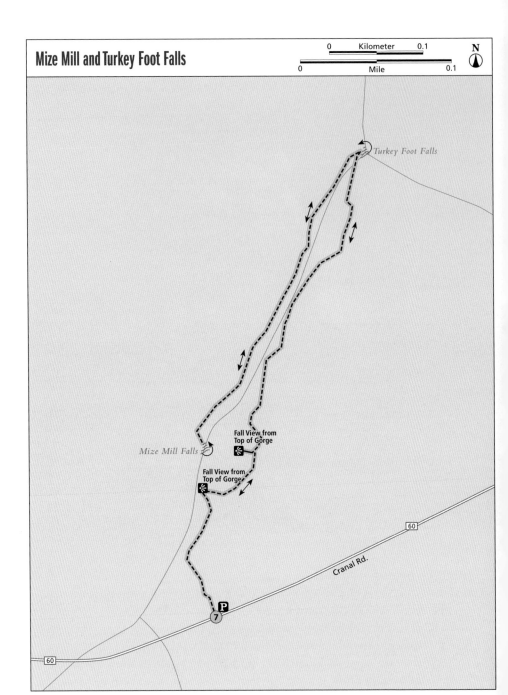

Mize Mill and Turkey Foot Falls

Turkey Foot Falls

Mize Mill Falls

Fall View from
Top of Gorge

Fall View from
Top of Gorge

Cranal Rd.

60

60

P

7

Miles and Directions

0.0 Start by crossing the highway from where you parked to the north. You can already hear Mize Mill Falls from here. There is an unmarked but fairly well-worn dirt and gravel path that begins heading downhill. In 200 feet, turn right at the creek. In less than 0.1 mile you will get your first chance to see the falls from a side trail to your left.

0.1 Another view of Mize Mill Falls off a side trail. Continue to the northeast on the narrow, rocky footpath along the rim of the canyon. In less than 0.1 mile, climb 50 feet down on the rock- and root-strewn trail to reach the bottom of the canyon. At the bottom, turn right (north) onto a nondescript trail.

0.2 Cross the creek and arrive at the base of the plunge Turkey Foot Falls. When ready, walk up the creek (south) on the opposite side from where you came down.

0.4 Pass an established campsite and arrive at Mize Mill Falls. When ready, turn around and retrace your steps to the trailhead.

0.8 Arrive back at the trailhead.

Another impressive plunge waterfall, Turkey Foot Falls is accentuated with brilliant green moss.

8 Caney Creek Falls

Arguably the most photographed, visited, and recognizable waterfall in the state is Caney Creek Falls in the Bankhead National Forest. This beautiful 30-foot punch-bowl waterfall pours down over the top of a rock shelter where you can walk under and behind the curtain of water. The falls culminates in a beautiful turquoise pool below. The waterfall is spectacular any time of the year—in spring, it is framed by brilliant mountain laurel; in fall, the fiery colors of autumn illuminate the scene; in winter, the spray sometimes freezes, holding the falls in suspended animation; and in summer, it's a great swimming hole.

Height of falls: 30 feet
Type of falls: Punchbowl
Distance: 2.0 miles out and back
Difficulty: Easy with a short, moderate switch-back to the falls
Hiking time: About 1 hour
Start: From the north side of the parking lot at the metal gate
Trail surface: Rutted gravel road, dirt footpath, rocks heading down to falls
Best seasons: Year-round; open sunrise–sunset
Canine compatibility: Dogs permitted; leash required

Fees and permits: None
County: Winston
Land status: National forest
Trail contact: Bankhead National Forest, Bankhead Ranger District, 1070 Hwy. 33, Double Springs; (205) 489-5111; www.fs .usda.gov/detail/alabama/about-forest/ districts/?cid=fsbdev3_002553
Maps: *DeLorme: Alabama Atlas & Gazetteer:* Page 23, C10
Special considerations: See details in the hike text about parking issues that have been encountered here.

Finding the trailhead: From Double Springs, at the intersection of US 278 and AL 33, take US 278 east 0.2 mile and turn right onto AL 195/Haleyville Road. Travel 5.9 miles and turn right onto CR 2. Travel 1.7 miles. The small parking area will be on your left. See more info in the hike text. Trailhead GPS: N34 14.113' / W87 26.041'; Falls GPS: N34 14.781' / W87 25.977'

The Hike

As mentioned earlier, Caney Creek Falls is arguably the most photographed waterfall in the state, which means only one thing—in the spring and summer months, this waterfall can be very crowded. Don't let that deter you, just be patient and share the trail. But, having said that, parking has become an issue.

The parking area is a small dirt pull-off on CR 2 with room for maybe ten tightly packed cars, if that many. The land surrounding the parking area is private property, but the landowners have generously allowed hikers to park here within a taped-off area.

One of the most photographed waterfalls in the state—Caney Creek.

Sometimes, so many people visit the falls that the road is jammed with cars blocking the road for first responders, which results in ticketing and towing of vehicles. Landowners have threatened to close this access to the falls.

Help keep this access point open by being courteous to the landowners. If the parking area is packed with cars when you arrive, consider visiting another waterfall in the forest and come back to Caney another day.

OK, enough of that, let's get to the hike. The path starts at a steel pipe gate that blocks traffic from traveling down the gravel and dirt road that makes up most of the trail. Simply walk around the gate to begin your trek.

The hike is relatively easy along this old, rutted road, which eventually narrows to a 2- to 3-foot-wide dirt footpath. This section is simply a nice walk in the woods with a few red cardinal plants dotting the trail.

At 0.9 mile, you will first hear the falls and then get a view from above. Here you will start heading downhill into the gorge using a series of switchbacks. Please stay on

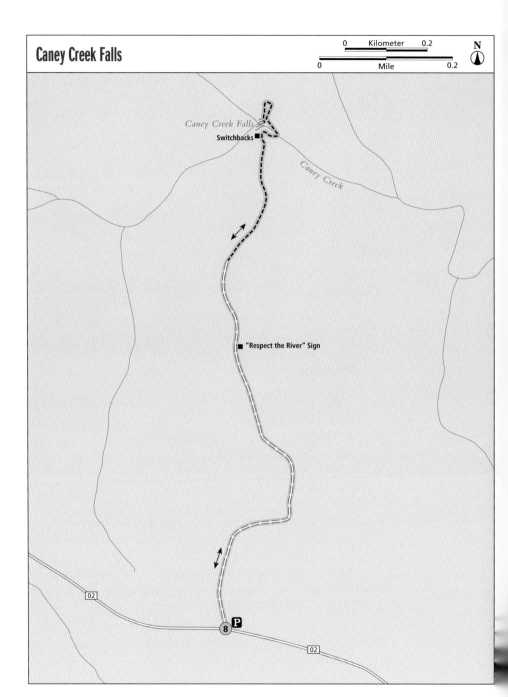

Caney Creek Falls

Caney Creek Falls
Switchbacks ■

Caney Creek

◆ "Respect the River" Sign

02

8 🅿

02

This big fella takes a break from the summertime heat in Caney Creek Falls's clear, cool pool.

the trail. Cutting across and heading straight down causes erosion that volunteers will have to repair. It's backbreaking work to say the least.

As you approach the bottom, use caution. The path narrows as it makes its way down the slippery rocks. At the bottom, the sound of the falls echoes off the canyon walls and is tremendous.

The trail is not blazed, but you will find it hard to get lost. The path is well worn. Optionally, you can cross the creek and follow it downstream a short distance to view the lower falls.

Miles and Directions

0.0   Start from the dirt and gravel parking lot to the north. Walk around the steel gate to the right. The path is a wide gravel and dirt road, heavily rutted due to erosion.

0.5   Pass a sign reminding you to "Respect the River."

0.7   The downhill walk to the falls begins. Shortly you will hear the falls in the distance.

0.8   Come to a Y intersection. The right fork is a cutoff that careless people have made to get to the falls quicker. Please don't use this (see the hike details). Take the left fork to the northwest and use the switchbacks downhill.

0.9   Come to a small rock overlook of the falls on the left. From here the switchbacks become narrow and very close to the edge. Use caution.

1.0   Arrive at the falls. When done exploring, retrace your steps to the trailhead.

2.0   Arrive back at the trailhead.

Bankhead National Forest and Sipsey Wilderness Honorable Mentions

A. Bee Branch Falls

If you're looking for a great overnight backpacking trip or maybe just a full day hike, then check out this hike to Bee Branch Falls in the Sipsey Wilderness. The 11.3-mile hike takes you through impressive boulder-strewn landscapes, past tall and moody, green moss-covered bluffs of the wilderness, culminating with a visit to Bee Branch Falls, a gorgeous 70-foot-tall ribbon plunge. You should really have orienteering skills (using map and compass—and be sure to bring them with you) because there are many game and social trails that branch off the main path, and since the trails are not blazed or numbered, it is easy to get off-track. Plus, GPS signals can be spotty in the heart of the wilderness.

The hike begins by following the same route as hike 4, Feather Hawk Falls, starting at the Randolph Trail trailhead and following Trail 202 for 2.9 miles to the Sipsey Fork. You can visit Feather Hawk first if you like, then at the intersection of the trail with the river, cross the river. It is "usually" an easy but wide crossing, but can be deep and swift during times of high water. Use your best judgment during those times and stay safe. Once on the other side, pick up Trail 209 (Sipsey River Trail) and follow it to the left (west) for 1.6 miles, passing Trail 204 on the way, then turn right (north) onto Trail 204A (East Bee Branch Trail). You'll wind your way through the canyon for 1.1 miles and arrive at the falls. When ready, turn around and retrace your steps back to the trailhead. Trailhead GPS: N34 17.279' / W87 28.283'; Falls GPS: N3419.706' / W87 26.705'

B. Eagle, Deer Skull, and Little Ugly Falls

Three waterfalls line up in a row on this 4-mile out-and-back hike in the Sipsey Wilderness, but you will have to work to get there. There are no established trails to these falls, so you need to bring along your GPS and a map and compass just to be on the safe side. First in line is the amazing 20-foot-tall, 30-foot-wide cascade called Eagle Falls. This is followed by the dual cascades of Deer Skull Falls, and finally the far from ugly 10-foot cascade Little Ugly.

To find the trailhead, follow the Finding the Trailhead directions in hike 5 (Borden Creek), but instead of parking at the Sipsey Recreation Area, continue down Cranal Road/CR 60 an additional 2.5 miles (passing Wolfpen Camp) and park in the dirt and gravel pull-off. There is room for three cars at most. From the parking area, start to the north on an old dirt road. In 300 feet the road forks. Take the left fork to the west, walking parallel to Cranal Road. From here on, the route can be dicey with blowdowns, brush, and drop-offs, so use caution. The road will narrow to a singletrack path, and at mile 0.2 it begins to swing to the northwest, eventually running into a creek bed that you can follow downhill until you reach the banks of Ugly Creek at mile 0.4. Turn right and follow the creek to the north. Eagle Falls will be on your left at mile 0.7. Continue to follow the creek north, picking the easiest path (you may find yourself crossing it several times or just walking down the creek). At mile 1.4 a feeder of the Sipsey Fork branches to the right. Continue following the creek to the left, and at mile 1.5 you will come to a feeder to the Sipsey Fork and Deer Skull Falls. Use caution and make your way across the stream to the far side of the right-most cascade. Once there, turn left and climb up the side of the canyon. Follow the creek bed for about 100 yards and arrive at Little Ugly Falls. When ready, retrace your steps back to the trailhead. Wild Alabama often offers hikes to these falls (see Appendix B: Additional Resources for their contact information). Parking GPS: N34 17.020' / W87 26.302'; Eagle Falls GPS: N34 17.364' / W87 26.736'; Deer Skull Falls GPS: N34 17.850' / W87 26.616'; Little Ugly Falls GPS: N34 17.838' / W87 26.652'

C. Braziel Creek Falls and Rock House

Hike the trail less traveled, Trail 207 (Braziel Creek Trail), to visit a beautiful, but very seasonal, 30-foot tiered cascade that crashes over its sandstone walls to a rock-strewn base and a spectacular 20-foot-tall rock shelter. By seasonal I mean this waterfall is nonexistent in summer.

Begin this hike at the Borden Creek trailhead. To find it, from the intersection of US 278 and AL 33 in Double Springs, take AL 33 north 12.6 miles. Turn left onto Cranal Road/CR 6 and travel 0.8 mile. Turn right onto the gravel Bunyan Hill Road/CR 5. The large gravel parking lot will be ahead in 2.2 miles. Park here and walk about 500 yards up the road to the gate that blocks the bridge over Borden Creek. Take the narrow dirt footpath downhill to the right of the bridge to the banks of the creek and turn right (northeast) heading upstream. In 0.2 mile, arrive at the junction of Trail 203 (Lookout Trail) and Trail 207. It's time to get your feet wet! Cross the 40-foot-wide Borden Creek to the north. The opposite bank is a steep, muddy 6-foot climb. Pick your way to find the easiest way up. Once on the other side, turn left onto Trail 207 and begin following Braziel Creek. At mile 1.6 you will pass Clifty Creek flowing into Braziel on the left. At mile 1.9, Trail 207 begins to move uphill away from the creek, until at mile 2.2 you will come to an intermittent stream. Clamber up the creek bed to the northeast, crossing the creek in 0.1 mile as you arrive at the waterfall. Follow the bluff line from the falls to the north, and in less than 0.1 mile (mile 2.4), you'll arrive at the Rock House. When ready, retrace your steps back to the trailhead. Trailhead GPS: N34 18.481' / W87 23.401'; Falls GPS: N34 19.827' / W87 23.799'

D. Sougahoagdee Falls

Sougahoagdee Falls is considered one of the Sipsey's most beloved waterfalls. This 70-foot-tall, wide curtain waterfall cascades down over a deep rock shelter into a bowl-shaped blue-green pool, the rock shelter allowing you to walk behind the curtain. This is a year-round waterfall that's best experienced in spring or early summer when rains are plentiful and the creek runs full. The greens of the moss and plants surrounding and beneath the falls are vibrant and really light up the hollow. And if you visit during rainy seasons, you will be treated to several additional unnamed cascades that form and tumble down the sandstone bluffs along the trail.

Sougahoagdee is accessible via an easy 4.5-mile out-and-back hike beginning at the Brushy Creek trailhead. To get to the trailhead, from Double Springs, at the intersection of AL 33 and US 278, take AL 33 north 8.4 miles and turn right onto AL 76. Travel 1.1 miles and bear right onto CR 63/Cheatham Road. Drive 1.5 miles and turn left onto Hickory Grove Road. The trailhead—a large gravel lot with plenty of room—will be ahead on the left just before crossing a bridge over Brushy Creek. The Brushy Creek Trail begins to the north then winds its way along the banks of the creek to this stunner of a waterfall. When ready, retrace your steps back to the trailhead. Parking GPS: N34 15.113' / W87 14.743'; Falls GPS: N34 15.254' / W87 15.888'

E. Wolfpen Falls

This is a 1.6-mile off-trail out-and-back hike in the Sipsey Wilderness. I've said it before but I'll say it one more time: Even though it is easy to find the waterfall once you hit the banks of Wolfpen Branch, you are still bushwhacking through the wilderness, and there are plenty of game trails and obstacles like downed trees and thick brush. You really need to bring along that map and compass just in case your GPS and cell phone lose reception. The reward for those who are comfortable with orienteering is this nice 15-foot cascade, Wolfpen Falls. This seasonal waterfall tumbles down a short sandstone rock shelter, crashing into its boulder-strewn base. And by seasonal I mean it does dry up pretty quickly in the drier months.

The hike begins at Wolfpen Cemetery on Cranal Road. To get to the trailhead, follow the instructions in the Finding the Trailhead section of hike 5 (Borden Creek), but instead of parking at the Sipsey Recreation Area, continue down the road to the west an additional 1.9 miles and park at the cemetery. A faint trail heads off to the north but disappears pretty quickly. Head north until you reach the banks of Wolfpen Branch where you will turn right (northeast) and follow the creek until you reach the falls at mile 0.8. You may have to zigzag across the branch a few times to find an easy path. Once you arrive at the falls, the easiest way down to the base is on the eastern side just past the falls, where it's pick your own way down, but use caution. It has some steep drop-offs. When ready, retrace your steps back to the trailhead. Trailhead GPS: N34 16.998' / W87 25.703'; Falls GPS: N34 17.398' / W87 25.723'

North Alabama

The waterfalls of the Bankhead National Forest and Sipsey Wilderness that we just explored are a subset of the north Alabama region. This region stretches across the state from the Mississippi to Georgia state lines and southward from Huntsville to just north of Birmingham.

Geologically speaking, this region is made up of the Highland Rim region with mountains, topping out at about 900 feet tall, that were formed some 323 to 353 million years ago. The bulk of the region, however, is part of the Cumberland Plateau.

Thousands of years ago, this entire region was covered by a shallow ocean. As the waters receded and the land began to rise, ancient shell banks and coral reefs dried out and died, leaving behind a bedrock of sandstone and limestone. Over the years, the action of the elements and the myriad creeks, streams, and rivers on the soft rock created huge crags, cliffs, and caves. You will see evidence of this in our hikes to the deepest canyon east of the Mississippi—the hike to Little River and Little Falls (hike 28), the unbelievable rock shelter that takes you behind the thundering water of Noccalula Falls (hike 35), and to one of my personal favorites, Cane Creek Canyon Nature Preserve in Tuscumbia (hike 11).

Cane Creek Canyon is a 400-acre preserve with myriad trails—over 15 miles, in fact—that wind down from a beautiful mountain vista called "The Point" into the canyon that has been carved by the elements and the preserve's namesake creek. The hike through the canyon takes you to towering rock bluffs, deep rock shelters, enumerable species of wildflowers, and many tall, tumbling waterfalls.

The erosion previously described created not only canyons, but also an amazing geologic phenomenon known as karst geology. Basically, karst is a process where surface water erodes the soft limestone underground and forms a distinct—and deep—hole in the ground (better known as a sinkhole). It also creates an intricate series of underground passages, a caver's delight. In Alabama the creeks that flow into these sinkholes are still at work today, giving us spectacular waterfalls with breathtaking beauty. We'll visit two of them on our journey—Lost Sink (hike 17) and Neversink Pit (hike 21).

A geologic, historic, and wildflower-strewn trail leads to Fagan Springs at Monte Sano Nature Preserve.

Rushing streams and breathtaking waterfalls are the focus of many of the other hikes that I have included in this section. Hikes through Shoal Creek Preserve (hike 9) and the Azalea Cascade, Laurel and Lost Falls Loop in DeSoto State Park (hike 25) showcase these fast-flowing creeks and cascades.

Hiking in the north region of the state is pleasant most of the year. Daytime winter temperatures average around 50°F during the day and 36 at night. For those who think that it doesn't snow in the South, think again. You will see some days with significant accumulations of snow and ice in this region throughout winter.

In the summer, expect averages of 90°F during the day and mid-70s at night. You will also experience the famous southern summertime humidity, which when combined with the already high air temperature makes for high heat indexes, sometimes in the triple digits, so prepare accordingly and bring plenty of water and sunscreen.

There are plenty of camping options, especially in the state parks that dot the region, including Joe Wheeler and two of the parks where we will visit a few waterfalls, Monte Sano and DeSoto. Visit www.alapark.com for complete details and to make reservations.

Time to explore the many waterfalls of north Alabama.

9 Shoal Creek Preserve

A beautiful walk in the woods can be had at the Alabama Forever Wild's Shoal Creek Preserve. You won't find a towering, thundering waterfall here, but instead you can relax next to a set of short, tranquil cascades along the preserve's Lawson Branch. Even though the tallest waterfall is a long but low 10–foot, two–tier cascade, the soothing sounds and sparkling waters combined with the solitude of the mixed hard-wood forest make this an amazing trip for families and nature lovers.

Height of falls: 10 feet
Type of falls: Double cascade
Distance: 4.3-mile double loop
Difficulty: Easy
Hiking time: About 2.5 hours
Start: From the trailhead kiosk on the north side of the parking lot
Trail surface: Hard-packed dirt footpath
Best seasons: Sept–May (see Special considerations); open sunrise–sunset
Canine compatibility: Dogs permitted; leash required
Fees and permits: None
County: Lauderdale

Land status: Alabama Forever Wild tract
Trail contact: Alabama State Lands, Alabama Department of Conservation and Natural Resources, 64 N. Union St., Montgomery, AL 36130; (334) 242-3484; www.alabama foreverwild.com/shoal-creek-preserve
Maps: *DeLorme: Alabama Atlas & Gazetteer.* Page 17, B8
Special considerations: Hunting is allowed in the preserve. Visit the Alabama State Lands website or call for dates, and be sure to wear orange. Horse trails intertwine with the hiking trail. Use caution.

Finding the trailhead: From Florence, at the intersection of US 72 (Florence Boulevard) and Darby Drive, head north 4.4 miles on Darby Drive/Old Jackson Highway. Turn left onto CR 61 (Butler Creek Road) and travel 2.6 miles. A small sign can be seen at the turn into the preserve on the right. Turn right and head down the gravel road 0.5 mile to the trailhead. Trailhead GPS: N34 54.449' / W87 37.240'; Falls GPS: N34 54.821' / W87 36.792'

The Hike

The next stop on our journey to the waterfalls of Alabama takes us to a small preserve just north of Florence—Shoal Creek Preserve.

This hike through the 298-acre preserve uses two trails—the red-blazed Jones Branch Loop and the double red–blazed Lawson Branch Loop. Both trails also have diamond-shaped trail markers tacked to trees.

Although I describe this as a 4.3-mile double loop, you can shorten the trek down to a 2.8-mile loop with a tail and still visit the main cascades (see the option in Miles and Directions).

Overall, this is an easy hike with nice views of Indian Camp Creek in the winter when the leaves are down as it flows into Shoal Creek. The hike is brightened

Not the most spectacular waterfall in the state, but this tiered cascade at Shoal Creek Preserve is the epitome of solitude.

in spring and summer with a variety of wildflowers growing along the edges of the woods at powerlines and, of course, our reason for being here, those cascades. Both are located on the Lawson Branch Loop. The tallest is a double cascade, each about 5 feet tall, cascading down a horseshoe-shaped rock bed. It is a tranquil spot to just sit and reflect. A smaller cascade will also be passed along this trail.

Remember, a horse trail weaves its way through the preserve as well, crossing the hiking trail several times. Watch for equestrians at crossings.

Miles and Directions

0.0 Start at the information kiosk on the north side of the parking lot. The trail begins on the left side of the kiosk. Immediately it splits into two trails. Take the left to begin the Jones Branch Loop.

0.4 Cross the horse trail to the north.

0.7 Arrive at Lawson Branch. Cross the branch over a bridge. On the other side, turn left onto the Lawson Branch Loop.

1.4 Views of Indian Camp Creek to the left.

1.5 Cross a runoff over a short footbridge.

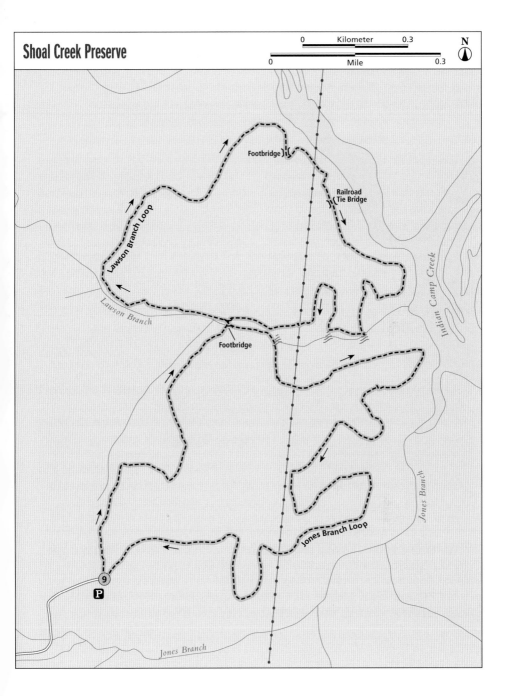

Shoal Creek Preserve

Footbridge

Railroad
Tie Bridge

Lawson Branch Loop

Lawson Branch

Footbridge

Indian Camp Creek

Jones Branch

Jones Branch Loop

9
P

Jones Branch

N

Kilometer
0   0.3
0   0.3
Mile

1.6 Cross a railroad tie footbridge over a runoff.

2.0 Come to a T intersection with the horse trail. Turn left onto the horse trail. In a few feet turn right (south) off the horse trail and continue on the Lawson Branch Loop. In less than 0.1 mile, there will be a cascade to the left.

2.1 Arrive at the double 5-foot cascade in a horseshoe-shaped rock bed in the creek.

2.3 Cross under a powerline with lots of wildflowers in the grass in spring.

2.4 Come to a Y intersection. Take the right fork to the west. In less than 0.1 mile, arrive back at the bridge over Lawson Branch. Cross it to the south, and on the other side turn to the left (east) onto the Jones Branch Loop. In less than 0.1 mile, turn left (south) onto an old dirt road. In 20 feet turn right (south) and continue on the Jones Branch Loop.

3.3 The trail skirts the eastern edge of the powerline.

3.4 As you approach trees along the powerline, the trail turns left (northeast) back into the woods (you will see the blaze).

3.7 The trail skirts the edge of the powerline again on its east side. There are wildflowers here.

3.8 Cross under the powerline to the west and head back into the woods.

4.3 Arrive back at the trailhead

Option: To make this a shorter 2.8-mile hike, after crossing the bridge at mile 0.7, turn to the right onto the Lawson Branch Loop. In 0.3 mile arrive at the horseshoe cascade mentioned at mile 2.1. Continue an additional 0.1 mile and arrive at the second cascade described at mile 2.0. When ready, retrace your steps back to this bridge and pick up the directions at mile 2.4.

Each year, Alabama receives a large sum of money from offshore oil and natural gas wells located off its coast in the Gulf of Mexico. In 1992 the state came up with a plan to put a small percentage of the interest earned from that drilling revenue aside and begin a new program that would preserve and protect land and water resources that have environmental or historical significance, and open that land wherever possible to the public for recreational use such as hunting, fishing, paddling, horseback riding, and, of course, hiking. The program was called Forever Wild. The plan went before voters in 1992, and by an almost unanimous vote, the program was born. Since that vote the program has purchased more than 200,000 acres of land and wetlands, and the acreage keeps growing. To learn more about Forever Wild, visit its website at www.alabamaforeverwild.com. There you will find an interactive map of the land under its protection and discover additional hiking trails across the state.

10 Wilson Dam Waterfall

A great hike for families with small children and those with disabilities to see a 45-foot cascade waterfall. This paved hike features beautiful, panoramic views of the Tennessee River, a great view of a classic neoclassical-style dam—Wilson Dam, a children's playground, restrooms, and, of course, a pretty cool cascade that flows down the rock cliff.

Height of falls: 45 feet
Type of falls: Cascade
Distance: 0.8 mile out and back
Difficulty: Easy
Hiking time: About 30 minutes
Start: At the east side of the parking lot
Trail surface: Paved (ADA accessible)
Best seasons: Year-round; open sunrise–sunset
Canine compatibility: Dogs permitted; leash required

Fees and permits: None
County: Lauderdale
Land status: Tennessee Valley Authority (TVA) property
Trail contact: Tennessee Valley Authority, SB1H, PO Box 1010, Muscle Shoals, AL 35661; (256) 386-2543; www.tva.gov/river/recreation
Maps: *DeLorme: Alabama Atlas & Gazetteer.* Page 17, D7; additional maps available on the TVA website
Special considerations: None. Just have fun.

Finding the trailhead: From Tuscumbia, at the intersection of US 43 and US 72, take US 43 north 3.9 miles and turn right onto Wilson Dam Highway. Travel 2.7 miles and Wilson Dam Highway becomes Reservation Road. Continue on Reservation Road 0.6 mile and turn left onto Rock Pile Road; follow it for 0.5 mile to the parking area, which has plenty of parking and is located near a boat ramp. The trailhead is on the east side of the parking lot. Trailhead GPS: N34 47.543 / W87 38.145'; Falls GPS: N34 47.645 / W87 37.587'

The Hike

Begin this hike on the eastern end of the parking lot at the TVA Rockpile Recreation Area. There is plenty of parking, but keep in mind that there is also a boat ramp here, so it could get crowded with anglers on weekends.

This is a nice walk over a paved path, perfect for families with small children and those with disabilities. Along the route you'll have a couple of good views of the wide Tennessee River. Only a few hundred feet into the trip, you will pass a set of restrooms, and 0.1 mile from the trailhead, a playground is on the right.

The waterfall is only a scant 0.4 mile from the trailhead. Be sure to stand behind the railing that protects visitors from slipping into the hole between the trail and the cliff.

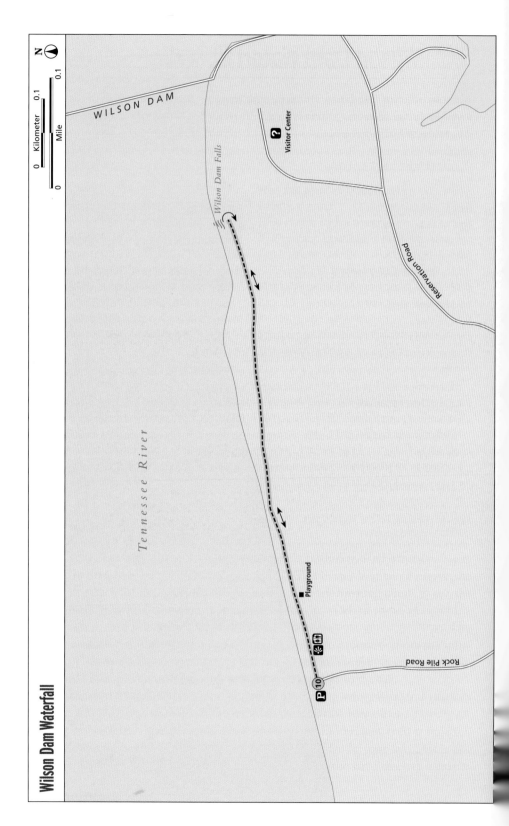

Wilson Dam Waterfall

WILSON DAM

Wilson Dam Falls

Tennessee River

Visitor Center

Reservation Road

Playground

Rock Pile Road

P 10

0   Kilometer   0.1

0   Mile   0.1

N

Miles and Directions

0.0 Start from the east side of the parking lot. In 500 feet, pass an overlook on the left. There are restrooms here.

0.1 Pass a playground on the right.

0.4 Arrive at the waterfall on the right. When ready, turn around and retrace your steps to the trailhead.

0.8 Arrive back at the trailhead.

A short, ADA-accessible walk along the Tennessee River at Wilson Dam leads to this beautiful walkway cascade. PHOTO COURTESY MARY CARTON

11 Cane Creek Canyon Nature Preserve

There is so much to explore at the Cane Creek Canyon Nature Preserve that you'll find yourself coming back time and time again. The 7-mile hike described here will lead you to spectacular bluffs, brilliant wildflowers in season, and walks beneath and around five waterfalls that roar down over rock shelters.

Height of falls: Various
Type of falls: Plunge and cascade
Distance: 7.0-mile loop
Difficulty: Moderate
Hiking time: About 3 hours
Start: From the parking lot just south of the Lacefield's house
Trail surface: Dirt, rock, some gravel
Best seasons: Year-round; open 7 a.m.–5 p.m.
Canine compatibility: Dogs permitted; leash required
Fees and permits: None
County: Colbert

Land status: Private, Nature Conservancy managed
Trail contact: Friends of Cane Creek, 251 Loop Rd., Tuscumbia; (256) 381-6301; www.facebook.com/Friends-of-Cane-Creek-Canyon -Nature-Preserve-126802417335447/
Maps: *DeLorme: Alabama Atlas & Gazetteer.* Page 17, E6; additional maps available at registration
Special considerations: You must sign the register at the parking area before heading out and when leaving the preserve.

Finding the trailhead: From Tuscumbia, at the intersection of US 72 and Veterans Boulevard, take US 72 west 0.7 mile and turn left onto CR 65/Frankfort Road. Travel 7.6 miles and turn right onto Loop Road. In 0.2 mile, as Loop Road bends to the right, continue straight on a gravel road (a sign points the direction to the preserve). Travel 0.3 mile, passing a poultry farm on the left, and through a gate indicating the entrance to the preserve until you come to a Spanish-influenced house. This is the Lacefield's home. You will see signs plainly indicating where to park. Trailhead GPS: N34 37.332' / W87 47.668'; Falls GPS: several scattered along the trail

The Hike

The 7-mile hike described here is only one of many possible routes through the preserve. There are over 18 miles of trail that loop through the property and interconnect.

The property is owned by Jim and Faye Lacefield, who live on the land, which is managed by The Nature Conservancy. You will start the hike just south of the Lacefield's home near the parking area. You are required to sign a register before beginning your hike so they can track who is on the trail. And don't forget to sign out before you leave.

The hike is rated moderate because of its length and the climb out of the canyon. It's not too difficult, but it is still a climb.

While the paths are not blazed, intersections are well marked with signs. For your convenience, vault toilets are scattered about the trails as well as water jugs filled with water in case you need a refill.

The trail is a combination of dirt and rock footpaths that lead to five waterfalls. Before you get to the falls, however, you get to see an expansive and breathtaking view of the canyon and surrounding mountains from "The Point."

The first waterfall comes as you head down a series of stairs only 0.3 mile into the hike. This one is at the rim of the canyon, so be very careful. As you cross a narrow footbridge to the south, you will get a better view.

To me, the best waterfalls come at the halfway point of the hike, just as you begin the trip back to the trailhead. It is in an area known as Devil's Hollow. Here you will encounter three stunning falls—Johnson, Yellow Wood, and Karen's Falls. From there, you'll get some amazing photo ops as you walk beneath enormous rock bluffs that hang out over the appropriately named Under Bluff Trail before passing Malone Branch Falls and returning to the trailhead.

Right out of the gate you meet your first of many waterfalls at Cane Creek Canyon.

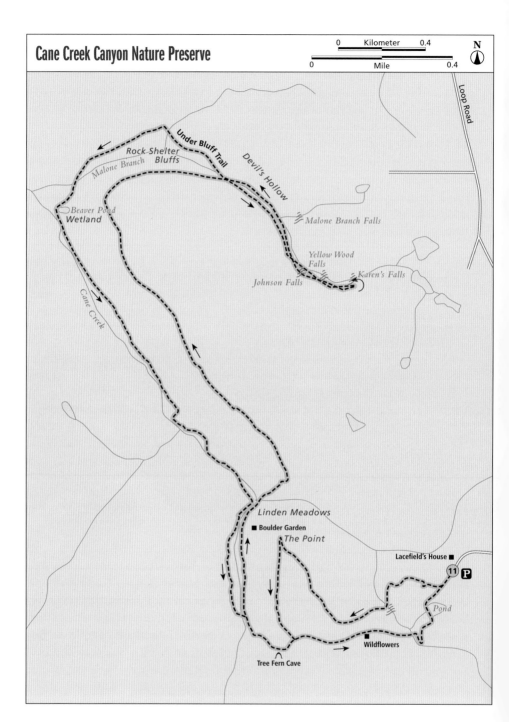

Cane Creek Canyon Nature Preserve

0 Kilometer 0.4

0 Mile 0.4

N

Loop Road

Under Bluff Trail

Rock Shelter Bluffs

Malone Branch

Devil's Hollow

Malone Branch Falls

Beaver Pond Wetland

Yellow Wood Falls

Karen's Falls

Johnson Falls

Cane Creek

Linden Meadows

■ Boulder Garden

The Point

Lacefield's House ■

11 P

Pond

Wildflowers

Tree Fern Cave

Miles and Directions

0.0   Start at the parking lot at the Lacefield's house. Take the dirt road 250 feet. Take the right fork at the Y intersection, passing a vault toilet on the left in a few yards.

0.2   Arrive at "Small Point" with three restrooms and a campsite. Take the Waterfall Trail down a series of stairs.

0.3   Come to a waterfall and rock shelter. Cross a narrow footbridge to the south and take the left fork of the Y uphill (west).

0.4   Take the right fork onto the Canyon Rim Trail.

0.8   Arrive at "The Point." Take the right fork of a Y to the south on the Canyon Rim Trail.

1.1   Come to a T intersection and turn right (southeast) onto the wide path and in less than 0.1 mile, take the right fork of a Y (southwest). In less than 0.1 mile, pass through a metal gate. In a few yards, arrive at the Tree Fern Cave Rock Shelter.

1.3   Come to a Y. Take the right fork onto the East Cane Creek Trail.

1.6   Turn right onto a small trail at the Boulder Garden sign to loop around the two big boulders and wildflowers.

1.7   Turn right to continue on the East Cane Creek Trail and in less than 0.1 mile, pass Linden Meadows on the left. Pick up the Shelf Trail in less than 0.1 mile.

3.5   Arrive at Johnson Falls on the right.

3.7   Come to Yellow Wood Rock Shelter and Falls. Continuing to the east, arrive at Karen's Falls. Cross the creek and pick up the Under Bluff Trail on the other side.

4.1   Pass Malone Branch Falls on the right.

4.8   Pass an old beaver pond and a tranquil wetland. Head south on the main Cane Creek Trail.

5.4   Turn right (southwest) onto the East Cane Creek Trail.

5.8   Back at the Y at mile 1.7, continue straight to the southwest. In a few yards turn left and cross Cane Creek and arrive at the Linden Meadows picnic area. Turn right (southwest) onto the West Cane Creek Trail.

6.1   Take the right fork of a Y onto the South Boundary Road.

6.4   Continue straight on South Boundary Road.

6.5   Pass a wildflower patch.

7.0   Arrive back at the first Y intersection, from the beginning of the hike. Continue straight to the northeast and the parking lot. In less than 0.1 mile, arrive back at the parking lot/trailhead.

12 Dismals Canyon

The tall, moss-covered sandstone walls of Dismals Canyon offer hikers a chance to view two waterfalls as well as incredible geology. The hike around the bottom of the canyon leads you to and through breathtaking geologic features including house-size boulders, caves and rock shelters, and, of course, those waterfalls—the 15-foot Rainbow Falls and 8-foot Secret Falls. Oh, and a truly "phantom" waterfall. The hike is an easy walker, and your kids will love exploring all of the nooks and crannies of the canyon.

Height of falls: Rainbow Falls, 15 feet; Secret Falls, 8 feet
Type of falls: Cascade
Distance: 1.1 miles out and back with 2 loops
Difficulty: Easy
Hiking time: About 1 hour
Start: From the back deck of the park's general store and restaurant
Trail surface: Rock, sand, short bit of stairs
Best seasons: Year-round; open 10 a.m.–5:30 p.m. Mon–Thurs, 10 a.m.–7 p.m. Fri, 9 a.m.–9 p.m. Sat, 9 a.m.–5 p.m. Sun
Canine compatibility: Dogs permitted; leash required

Fees and permits: Day-use fee
County: Franklin
Land status: Conservatory
Trail contact: Dismals Canyon, 901 Hwy. 8, Phil Campbell, AL 35581; (205) 993-4559; www.dismalscanyon.com/thecanyon
Maps: DeLorme: Alabama Atlas & Gazetteer: Page 23, B6; canyon map available online or at the park's store
Special considerations: There are numerous "squeezes" (some as narrow as 1 to 2 feet wide) that may not be appropriate for the claustrophobic.

Finding the trailhead: From the intersection of AL 13 and AL 237 in Phil Campbell, take AL 237 0.5 mile. Turn right onto CR 12/College Road. Travel 3.2 miles and turn left onto US 43 South. In 1.1 miles turn right onto CR 8. Travel 0.9 mile. The entrance to the park will be on your left. Turn into the entrance and you will immediately be in the small parking lot. Park and head to the country store. After paying your fee and signing a liability waiver inside the store, you will begin the hike through two French doors in the left center of the building. Trailhead GPS: N34 19.568' / W87 46.907'; Falls GPS: Rainbow Falls, N34 19.506' / W87 46.922'; Secret Falls, N34 19.406' / W87 46.887'

The Hike

The trail itself through Dismals Canyon is a narrow, rock-strewn footpath that leads you through and under tall rock bluffs and shelters where Native Americans once lived centuries ago and bandits used to hide.

The two waterfalls on this hike are cascades, tumbling down large boulders. The first, and the centerpiece of the hike, comes at just about 0.1 mile into the trek— Rainbow Falls. This 15-foot cascade is formed by a dam, the force of the water at one time powering an old mill that was once located here. You will see the old mill stones at the bottom of the falls.

Immediately as you begin the hike into Dismals Canyon, you are greeted by Rainbow Falls.

The second waterfall is an 8-foot cascade that is aptly named Secret Falls. This waterfall is hidden off the main trail at about 0.7 mile into the hike and is formed by an underground spring that pops aboveground some 0.75 mile upstream. The park calls the area around the falls a natural arboretum, with twenty-seven species of native trees growing within 100 feet of it.

Trail maps show that there is a third waterfall—Phantom Falls—but it is just that. The sound of Rainbow Falls crashing down to the canyon floor echoes off the rock walls, making you think there is another waterfall nearby.

Dismals Canyon is steeped in history beginning with its geologic roots that date back over 300 million years ago during what is known as the Paleozoic Era, when the land lifted up, an ancient primordial swamp drained, and the resulting action of the water flowing through the rock weathered it away to form the gorge you see today. The first human inhabitants, Paleo-Americans, arrived around 10,000 years ago and left behind a fairly complete record of their past through spear points and other relics. Later Native Americans, including Chickasaw and Cherokee, called this canyon home as well. In 1838 a tragic chapter of the infamous "Trail of Tears" was played out here when US soldiers rounded up the Chickasaw and interned them in the canyon for two weeks before "herding them off like cattle" to Muscle Shoals and eventually to land west of the Mississippi. In all, 90 percent of the Chickasaw who were forcibly relocated died during the Trail of Tears.

It is said that when water falls over or seeps through Weeping Bluff, it's nature crying over the plight of her only friends—Native Americans.

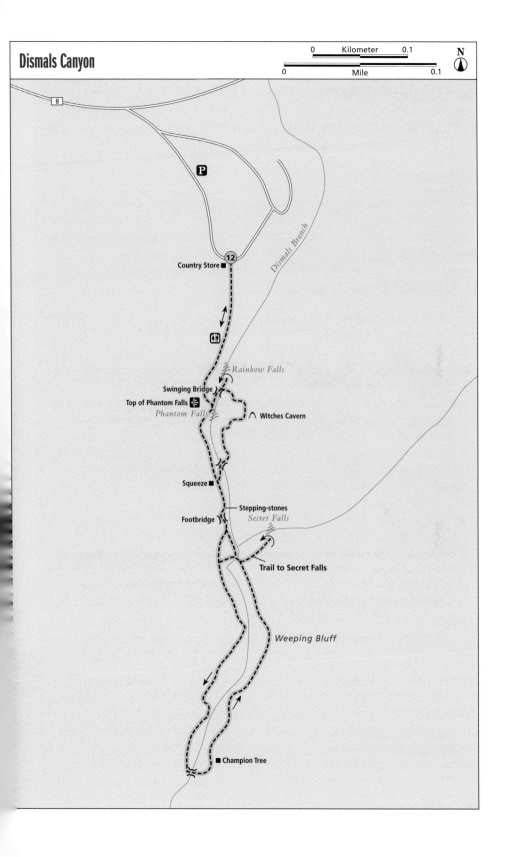

Dismals Canyon

0　Kilometer　0.1

0　Mile　0.1

N

8

P

12 Country Store ■

Dismals Branch

Rainbow Falls

Swinging Bridge

Top of Phantom Falls

Phantom Falls

∧ Witches Cavern

Squeeze ■

Stepping-stones

Secret Falls

Footbridge

Trail to Secret Falls

Weeping Bluff

■ Champion Tree

On your way to Secret Falls, at mile 0.4, you will come to a very picturesque scene. Here a wooden footbridge crosses a tranquil pool beneath the towering rock wall called "Weeping Bluff," where they say that if you look at the wall at the right angle you will see the face of an Indian maiden. The water seeping down the rock face makes it look as if she's crying. Locals say that the wall is crying for the loss of the canyon's only true friend, the Native Americans.

Miles and Directions

0.0 Start by passing through the French doors within the country store; head downhill on the stairs and cement walkway.

0.1 Arrive at the gorge and the base of Rainbow Falls on your left. In less than 0.1 mile, pass a swinging bridge across the creek on the left. Continue straight (south).

0.2 Come to a side trail on the right that leads to the top of Phantom Falls. When done visiting, continue straight to the south.

0.3 The path Ys. Take either fork around an outcropping. The left fork takes you through a narrow "squeeze." Where the two paths reconnect, there is a three-way intersection. Take either the middle or right fork.

0.4 View of "Weeping Bluff" across the creek.

0.5 Cross a footbridge over the creek and on the other side turn left (north). This is the return trip on the opposite side of the creek.

0.6 Take the right fork of the Y to visit the Champion Tree. Just past the tree there will be a set of stairs that lead back to the creek. Turn right and in less than 0.1 mile, walk through stone cuts. A set of 4-by-4-inch water-bar stairs lead the way.

0.7 Cross a wooden bridge below Weeping Bluff followed by a rock jumble (pass it to the left). In less than 0.1 mile, come to a side trail to the right to visit Secret Falls.

0.8 After viewing, retrace your steps to the main trail and turn right (north). In less than 0.1 mile cross eight stepping-stones over the creek.

0.9 Cross a short footbridge through another "squeeze." Cross a 50-foot bridge across the creek. On the other side make an immediate left (north).

1.0 Come to the "Witches Cavern." Keep walking straight until you run headlong into the rock wall. Turn to the right and walk through the narrow passageway. At the end, make a left and cross a swinging bridge. On the other side you are back at Rainbow Falls. Turn right and retrace your steps to the store.

1.1 Arrive back at the store and trailhead.

13 Walls of Jericho

Many words have been written about the Walls of Jericho—beautiful, awesome, amazing, stunning. They are all true. Along this 6.4-mile out-and-back hike, you will encounter deep sinkholes and caves, and cross beautiful turquoise streams before arriving at your destination, the Walls of Jericho—a spectacular, high-walled limestone bowl canyon with an incredible plunge waterfall on top that cascades into a hole in the rocks and eventually shoots out through the bottom tier of rocks far below.

Height of falls: Upper, 30 feet; lower, 15 feet
Type of falls: Upper, plunge; lower, cascade
Distance: 6.4 miles out and back
Difficulty: Difficult
Hiking time: About 5 hours
Start: At the hiker trailhead on CR 79
Trail surface: Dirt and rock footpath
Best seasons: Sept–June; open sunrise–sunset
Canine compatibility: Dogs permitted; leash required
Fees and permits: None
County: Jackson
Land status: Alabama Forever Wild property
Trail contact: Alabama State Lands, Alabama Department of Conservation and Natural

Resources, 64 N. Union St., Montgomery, AL 36130; (334) 242-3484; www.alabamaforeverwild.com/walls-jericho
Maps: DeLorme: Alabama Atlas & Gazetteer. Page 20, A3
Special considerations: The Walls are prone to flash flooding. The climb up the rock wall to the upper pool is steep and slippery, so use caution. And remember, what goes down must come up. It can be a very strenuous walk out of the canyon for some. Allow yourself plenty of time to get back to the trailhead before nightfall.

Finding the trailhead: From Scottsboro, take AL 79 north 26 miles. You will pass the Walls of Jericho equestrian trailhead on the left. Just after that the hiker trailhead will be on the left. If you cross over into Tennessee, you've gone too far. Trailhead GPS: N34 58.580 / W86 04.820'; Falls GPS: N34 59.456' / W86 06.242'

The Hike

Next to Caney Creek Falls (hike 8), the Walls of Jericho is arguably the most hiked destination in the state, and for good reason—so much to see and experience, and it's not only the waterfall. The hike leads you past deep sinkholes, across beautiful turquoise streams, and, of course, to the Walls itself—a huge, 200-foot-tall limestone amphitheater with an incredible waterfall.

Full disclosure—the Walls of Jericho is actually in Tennessee and not Alabama. You will cross the state line just before arriving at the amphitheater, but we're going to call it our own. Just don't tell anybody.

Walls of Jericho

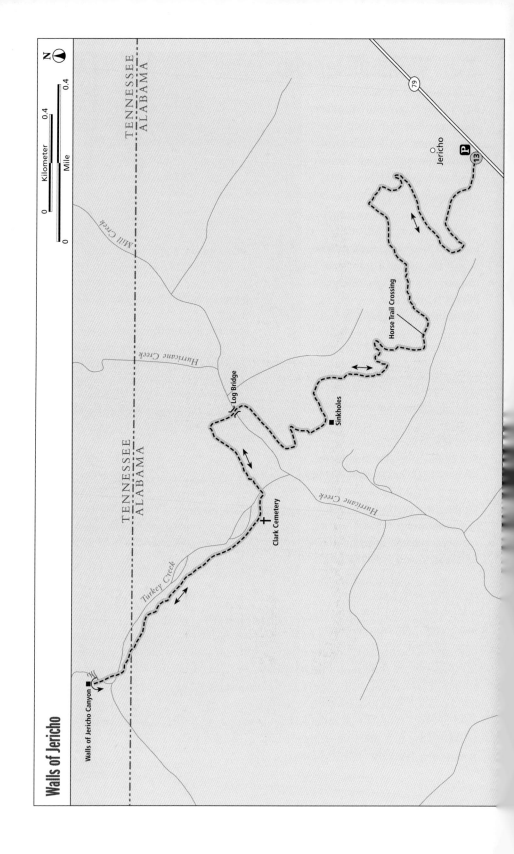

Walls of Jericho Canyon

Turkey Creek

Clark Cemetery

Log Bridge

Sinkholes

Horse Trail Crossing

Mill Creek

Hurricane Creek

Hurricane Creek

TENNESSEE
ALABAMA

TENNESSEE
ALABAMA

Jericho

P

79

13

N

Kilometer 0.4 0.4

Mile 0.4

The upper waterfall of the Walls of Jericho disappears into this limestone bowl only to reappear far below. PHOTO COURTESY DAVID PARHAM

As you enter the Walls, you will be greeted by the lower waterfall. This cascade flows down the rock wall from seemingly out of nowhere. After a good rain, the waterfall shoots out of the wall.

From here, climb up the rock ledge to the north, which will take you to the top of the canyon and the upper falls. This waterfall is a single ribbon that is channeled into a narrow hole with a deep pool. Use extra caution climbing to the upper falls. It is very steep and slippery.

While it is an easy walk down into the canyon, the hike out is another story. It is a 1,000-foot elevation gain, a difficult climb for many; plan extra time so that you can make it out of the canyon before sunset.

A primitive campsite has been established along the trail at mile 2.5 near the old Clark Cemetery from 1835. The campsite is free and available on a first-come, first-served basis, and has room for eight tents.

The trail uses red blazes as well as some yellow, diamond-shaped metal hiker markers. You will have a few streams to cross over footbridges; the one over the turquoise waters of Hurricane Creek at mile 2.2 uses a log that has been planed flat on one side and fitted with a handrail. You will also cross Turkey Creek over a footbridge at mile 3.0.

Miles and Directions

0.0 From the kiosk, cross the gravel equestrian trail and head west.

0.2 Start the descent into the canyon near a small creek.

0.6 Switchback downhill for the next 0.2 mile.

1.2 Cross the equestrian trail to the west, then cross a small creek shortly after.

1.8 Pass through stands of cane and sinkholes along the sides of the trail.

2.2 Cross Hurricane Creek over a log footbridge fitted with a handrail.

2.5 Rock-hop across a small feeder creek to Hurricane Creek and shortly arrive at Clark Cemetery and a camping area.

3.0 Cross Turkey Creek and arrive at the canyon. A cascade tumbles down the rocks to the left. Continue northwest into the canyon, carefully climbing up the rock wall of the bowl.

3.2 Arrive at the upper falls. When ready, turn around and retrace your steps to the trailhead.

6.4 Arrive back at the trailhead.

14 Fagan Springs

This short out-and-back hike at the Monte Sano Nature Preserve (the largest urban land preserve in the country) leads you to the seasonal Fagan Springs waterfall, an incredible block-type cascade that tumbles down a fascinating rocky bed that will keep you mesmerized. You can extend this trek into a 4.9-mile loop hike that connects the falls on Fagan Springs with Dry Falls (hike 15). See the option under Miles and Directions.

Height of falls: Tallest 15 feet
Type of falls: Cascade
Distance: 1.4 miles out and back
Difficulty: Moderate
Hiking time: About 1 hour
Start: On the south side of the hiker's parking lot off Bankhead Parkway NE
Trail surface: Dirt and rock footpath
Best seasons: Sept–May; open sunrise-sunset
Canine compatibility: Dogs permitted; leash required
Fees and permits: None

County: Madison
Land status: Land Trust of North Alabama preserve
Trail contact: Land Trust of North Alabama, 2707 Artie St. SW, Ste. 6, Huntsville, AL 35805; (256) 534-6141; www.landtrustnal.org
Maps: *DeLorme: Alabama Atlas & Gazetteer.* Page 19, D8; additional maps available on the land trust's website
Special considerations: The preserve can be crowded on weekends, so plan to arrive early.

Finding the trailhead: From I-565 at exit 21, Maysville Road NE, head south on Maysville Road NE 1.4 miles and turn left onto Pratt Avenue NE (Pratt Avenue becomes Bankhead Parkway NE in 400 feet). Travel 1.4 miles. The parking lot and trailhead will be on your right and is well marked. Trailhead GPS: N34 44.610' / W86 32.640'; Falls GPS: N34 44.369' / W86 32.767'

The Hike

This short out-and-back hike begins at the south side of the parking lot. The hike uses the Alms House Trail from the trailhead as well as the Fagan Springs Trail. With only a few exceptions, the trails are well blazed with metallic diamond markers.

Remember, this is another seasonal waterfall and the flow could be nonexistent in late summer. Sudden pop-up thunderstorms, however, will bring the falls to life at a moment's notice.

The hike begins with a moderate climb down a rocky bluff before bottoming out at a powerline where you will be treated to beautiful and fragrant wildflowers in season.

Within 0.5 mile, you will arrive at the Fagan Springs Trail and the main waterfall—a 15-foot-tall cascade over a picturesque rock bed. Continue an additional 0.2 mile to the intersection with the Wildflower Trail and you'll come to a second, smaller cascade.

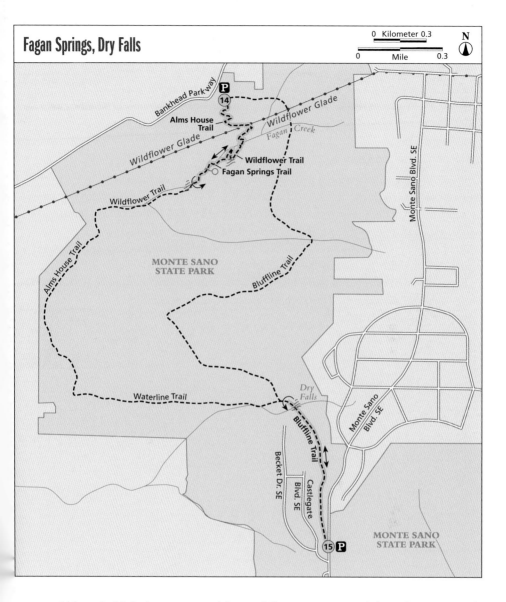

Fagan Springs, Dry Falls

0 Kilometer 0.3

0 Mile 0.3

N

Bankhead Parkway

Alms House Trail

Wildflower Glade

Wildflower Glade

Fagan Creek

Wildflower Trail

Fagan Springs Trail

Wildflower Trail

Alms House Trail

MONTE SANO STATE PARK

Bluffline Trail

Waterline Trail

Dry Falls

Bluffline Trail

Becket Dr. SE

Castlegate Blvd. SE

Monte Sano Blvd. SE

Monte Sano Blvd. SE

MONTE SANO STATE PARK

Although this is the turnaround for our hike, you can extend the trek to a 4.9-mile loop and add a visit to Dry Falls (hike 15). See option under Miles and Directions.

◄ *Fagan Springs courses down its craggy bed.*
Photo courtesy Melanie Manson, LTNA

Miles and Directions

0.0 Start from the south side of the parking lot on the Alms House Trail.

0.2 Cross under a powerline. There is a fragrant wildflower glade here in spring.

0.5 Come to an intersection. Turn right onto the Fagan Springs Trail and arrive at the main falls.

0.7 Come to a second, smaller waterfall on the Fagan Springs Trail. This will be the turnaround for the hike.

1.4 Arrive back at the trailhead.

Option: As mentioned, you can make this into a 4.9-mile loop that visits not only the falls at Fagan Springs but also Dry Falls (hike 15), while making stops at the remains of a historic springhouse (a stone structure that was built over a clear, cold stream to cool meats and vegetables) and Three Caves—an abandoned limestone quarry that, coincidentally enough, has three caves. You can't enter the caves, but they are an interesting sight. At mile 0.7 of this hike, instead of turning around, continue straight and connect the Wildflower Trail, Alms House Trail, and the steep Waterline Trail to reach Dry Falls. After viewing the falls, turn left (north) onto the Bluffline Trail and follow it back to the trailhead.

15 Dry Falls

Another waterfall hike in Huntsville's Monte Sano Nature Preserve is this easy 1-mile out-and-back walk that takes you to an impressive, towering rock bluff and a seasonal waterfall aptly named Dry Falls. When the streams are flowing, the cascade is impressive. You can take in both waterfalls in the preserve—Dry Falls and Fagan Springs (hike 14) with an extension of the Fagan Springs hike that will turn this into a 4.9-mile loop. See Miles and Directions under the Fagan Springs hike.

See map on page 57.
Height of falls: 50 feet
Type of falls: Plunge
Distance: 1.0 mile out and back
Difficulty: Easy
Hiking time: About 30 minutes
Start: At the hiker's parking lot on Monte Sano Boulevard SE
Trail surface: Dirt, rock
Best seasons: Fall–late spring; open sunrise–sunset
Canine compatibility: Dogs permitted; leash required

Fees and permits: None
County: Madison
Land status: Land Trust of North Alabama preserve
Trail contact: Land Trust of North Alabama, 2707 Artie St. SW, Ste. 6, Huntsville, AL 35805; (256) 534-5263; www.landtrustnal.org
Maps: *DeLorme: Alabama Atlas & Gazetteer:* Page 19, D8; additional maps available on the land trust's website
Special considerations: None. Just have fun.

Finding the trailhead: From Huntsville, at the intersection of US 231 and US 431/Governors Drive SW, take US 431/Governors Drive SW east 3.6 miles. Turn left onto Monte Sano Boulevard SE and travel 0.8 mile. The hiker's parking lot will be on the right. Carefully cross the road to the northwest to pick up the start of the Bluffline Trail. Trailhead GPS: N34 43.289' / W86 32.262'; Falls GPS: N34 43.715' / W86 32.412'

The Hike

This easy hike to Dry Falls is located on one of the oldest Land Trust of North Alabama tracts in the Huntsville area. The hike uses the southernmost section of the preserve's 2.5-mile-long Bluffline Trail. The trail is blazed with LTNA metal markers, but you would find it difficult to get lost on this well-worn path.

Begin the hike by carefully crossing Monte Sano Boulevard to the northwest from the hiker's parking lot. You will pick up the trail on the opposite side. From here it is an easy 0.5-mile walk to the intersection of the Bluffline and Waterline Trails, where one of the old main Huntsville waterlines was located, hence the name.

The bluff that the stream tumbles down will be on your right. The tall, flat sandstone wall is impressive in and of itself, but even more so after a good rain when the falls runs full. Remember, this is called Dry Falls for a reason. It is best to visit from

Dry Falls is appropriately named—sometimes it's dry, sometimes wet. When it's wet, it's dazzling. PHOTO COURTESY DAVID PARHAM

fall through spring when the rains fill the streambed, or after a typical southern summertime thunderstorm.

When you're ready, turn around and retrace your steps to the trailhead.

Miles and Directions

0.0 Start at the hiker's parking area and pick up the Bluffline Trail on the other side.

0.5 Arrive at Dry Falls, at the intersection of the Bluffline Trail and Waterline Trail. When ready, turn around and retrace your steps to the trailhead.

1.0 Arrive back at the trailhead.

16 Lodge and McKay Hollow Falls

Ramble along the ridge of Monte Sano Mountain in Huntsville to take in breathtaking views of the Rocket City's mountains and valleys and visit two little-known seasonal cascades that lurk just below the rim. We'll do a bit of bushwhacking down a creek bed to visit the multi-tiered cascade known as Lodge Falls, then hike a rugged (but short) section of the McKay Hollow Trail to view the plunge of McKay Hollow Falls.

Height of falls: Lodge Falls, 40 feet; McKay Hollow Falls, 40 feet
Type of falls: Lodge, tiered cascade; McKay Hollow, short plunge with long cascade
Distance: 1.0 mile out and back
Difficulty: Moderate
Hiking time: About 1 hour
Start: At the south side of the hiker's trailhead
Trail surface: Dirt and rock footpath
Best seasons: Late Sept–June; open 8 a.m.–sunset
Canine compatibility: Dogs permitted; leash required
Fees and permits: Day-use fee

County: Madison
Land status: Alabama state park
Trail contact: Monte Sano State Park, 5105 Nolen Ave., Huntsville, AL 35801; (256) 534-3757; www.alapark.com/parks/monte-sano-state-park
Maps: *DeLorme: Alabama Atlas & Gazetteer:* Page 19, D8; additional trail maps available at the park office
Special considerations: It is a rather steep downhill along the creek to Lodge Falls. Watch your footing on the loose rock along the McKay Hollow Trail, and watch where you put your hands—there could be snakes.

Finding the trailhead: From Huntsville, at the intersection of US 231 and US 431/Governors Drive SW, take US 431 east 3.6 miles and turn left onto Monte Sano Boulevard SE. Travel 2.4 miles and turn right onto Nolen Avenue SE. In 0.8 mile, come to the park entrance and pay your day-use fee. Continue straight on Nolen Avenue SE for 0.4 mile, making a slight right onto Bankhead Parkway NE. The hiker's parking area will be on the right with room for at least 40 cars. The hike begins at the south end of the parking area. Trailhead GPS: N34 44.570' / W86 31.050'; Lodge Falls GPS: N34 44.510' / W86 30.803'; McKay Hollow Falls GPS: N34 44.473' / W86 31.095'

The Hike

The blue-blazed North Plateau Loop at Monte Sano State Park is a nice walk around the rim of the park's namesake mountain, which has the nickname, the "Mountain of Health." Many people in the late 1800s/early 1900s believed the crisp mountain air was the tonic to cure all ills, including yellow fever.

Today Monte Sano is a great place to hike and get away from the bustle of the burgeoning city of Huntsville, and this trail will lead us to two little-known cascades that lie just below the rim of the mountain—Lodge Falls and McKay Hollow Falls.

This little gem—Lodge Falls—sits just below the summit of Monte Sano Mountain.
Photo courtesy David Parham

The North Plateau Loop is an easy walking trail that will take you to two incredible views of Huntsville Mountain. The first view comes at the park's lodge, the other at the intersection of the trail with the McKay Hollow Trail.

The first waterfall—Lodge Falls—is found just after crossing the Fire Tower Trail. There you will come to a creek, but before crossing it, you will turn off the trail to the south and follow the creek bed steeply downhill for less than 0.1 mile to arrive at the falls.

Continuing down the North Plateau Loop, you will come to the McKay Hollow Trail where you will find the falls of the same name. The trail heads steeply downhill to the south at the Civilian Conservation Corps (CCC) picnic pavilion, built in the 1930s. The trail is very difficult and rocky. Luckily, we will use only a short portion of it—about 200 feet or so—to get to the falls. As mentioned earlier, watch your step on the loose rock and keep an eye out for snakes sunning themselves. I have met a few here.

Along the rugged McKay Hollow Trail, you will find the second waterfall of this hike—McKay Hollow Falls. PHOTO COURTESY DAVID PARHAM

After admiring the cascade, turn around and retrace your steps to the trailhead. You can also extend the hike into a nice 1.9-mile loop (see option in Miles and Directions).

Miles and Directions

0.0 Start on the south side of the hiker's parking area and pick up the blue-blazed North Plateau Loop Trail. Head to the south. In less than 0.1 mile, pass the park's disc golf course hole 10. Watch for flying discs.

0.1 Cross the Fire Tower Trail to the southwest. Just after crossing, come to the Blue Spring creek bed. Turn off the trail and follow the creek steeply downhill and in less than 0.1 mile, arrive at Lodge Falls. When ready, climb back up to the trail and continue to the left (west).

0.3 Pass the park's lodge on the right with an expansive view to the left. In less than 0.1 mile, pass an amphitheater on the right.

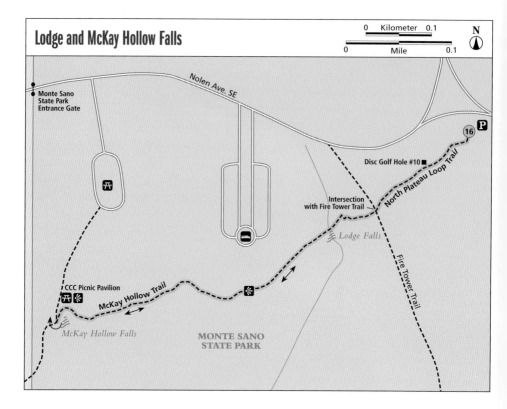

Lodge and McKay Hollow Falls

0.4 Cross a small creek and come to another overlook.

0.5 Arrive at the CCC picnic pavilion. Turn left (south) here onto the McKay Hollow Trail. In less than 0.1 mile, arrive at McKay Hollow Falls. When ready, turn around and retrace your steps to the trailhead.

1.0 Arrive back at the trailhead.

Option: Make this into a 1.9-mile loop by continuing on the North Plateau Loop to the west with more views and a visit to the Von Braun Observatory.

17 Lost Sink

A beautiful but rugged hike over rock slabs and boulders leads you up the side of Keel Mountain near Huntsville and this hidden gem—Lost Falls. This beautiful and picturesque 100-foot cascade tumbles down a limestone bluff where it disappears underground into a deep sinkhole.

Height of falls: 100 feet
Type of falls: Cascade
Distance: 2.2 miles out and back
Difficulty: Moderate
Hiking time: About 2 hours
Start: On the east side of the Keel Mountain Preserve at the information kiosk
Trail surface: Rock and dirt footpath
Best seasons: Sept–June; open sunrise–sunset
Canine compatibility: Dogs permitted; leash required
Fees and permits: None

County: Madison
Land status: Nature Conservancy preserve
Trail contact: The Nature Conservancy, 2100 1st Ave. N., Birmingham, AL 35203; (205) 251-1155; www.nature.org/en-us/about-us/ where-we-work/united-states/alabama/
Maps: *DeLorme: Alabama Atlas & Gazetteer.* Page 19, E10
Special considerations: The edge of the sink is extremely dangerous, with a precipitous drop. Use caution.

Finding the trailhead: From Huntsville, at the intersection of US 231 and US 431/Governors Drive SW, take US 431 south 11.6 miles and turn left onto Old Highway 431. Travel 2 miles and turn right onto Cherry Tree Road. Drive 2.2 miles and turn left onto McMullen Drive. Travel 1.2 miles. The parking area and trailhead will be on your right. The gravel parking area has room for 10 to 12 cars. The trailhead is on the east side of the parking lot. Trailhead GPS: N34 39.303' / W86 24.790'; Falls GPS: N34 39.776' / W86 24.935'

The Hike

Located only 11 miles as the crow flies (16 miles by car) southeast of Huntsville is the first of two incredible sinkhole waterfalls we will encounter on our journey across the state—Lost Sink.

The waterfall is located on a Nature Conservancy tract known as the Keel Mountain Preserve, a 310-acre preserve that was targeted for purchase by the Conservancy to protect the endangered Morefield leather flower. This vining plant produces large, purple bell-shaped flowers around June depending on the amount of rain, adding a splash of color to the dark greens of summer. So far, the plant has only been found in six areas, all of which are in the Huntsville area.

The hike begins alongside the cool, clear water and soothing sounds of Buck Ditch before it starts a moderate climb up and over rock slabs and boulders alternating with dirt footpaths to our destination. While it's a steady climb, average hikers

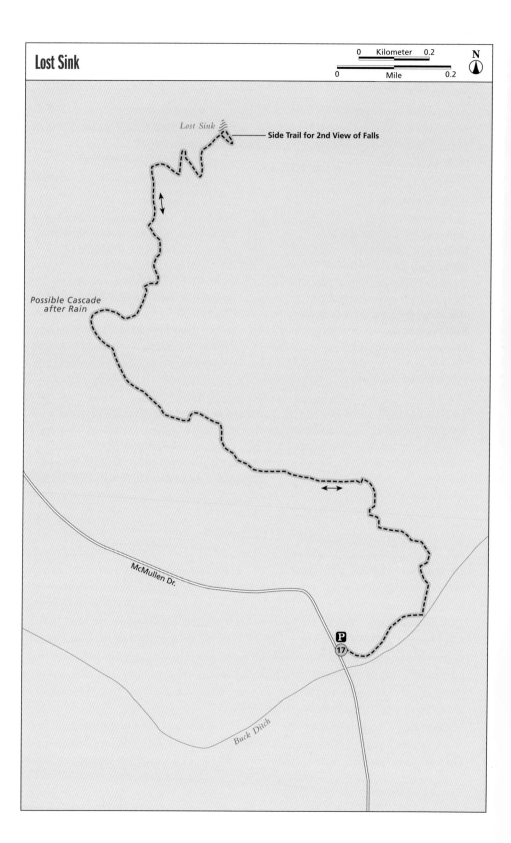

Lost Sink

0 Kilometer 0.2
0 Mile 0.2

N

Lost Sink
Side Trail for 2nd View of Falls

Possible Cascade
after Rain

McMullen Dr.

P
17

Buck Ditch

It is a breathtaking sight as this unnamed creek plummets into the deep sinkhole known as Lost Sink.

should be able to make the trek thanks to the many switchbacks and by taking your time and bringing plenty of water.

The trail is marked with green plastic diamond markers bearing yellow arrows pointing the direction of travel and the Nature Conservancy logo. While your eyes will be pointed down to watch your footing, be sure to keep an eye up in the trees for these markers. There are many game trails that can lead you off the path if you're not paying attention. I got off track at mile 1.0 just below the falls and had to backtrack to pick up the path again.

If you hike this trail in late spring and early summer, it sports a thick canopy that provides plenty of shade. Some areas of the trail retain water after a rain and become very muddy and slick. One particularly long area comes at mile 0.6. If you hike the trail just after a heavy rain, you may be treated to a second small cascade at mile 0.7, where you will cross a runoff over a rock ledge.

The view of the falls plunging into the deep sinkhole is breathtaking, but remember to use extreme caution around the rim. It is a precipitous drop to the bottom. Keep children and dogs away from the edge.

The trail actually continues to the north for a short distance from the falls, but for this description, this is our destination; turn around here and retrace your steps to the trailhead.

Miles and Directions

0.0 Start at the information kiosk on the east side of the parking lot. Buck Ditch flows next to this section of the trail.

0.2 The trail begins to switchback steeply up the mountain.

0.7 Cross a runoff that may have a nice cascade flowing off a ledge following heavy rain.

1.1 Arrive at the falls. When ready, turn around and retrace your steps to the trailhead.

2.2 Arrive back at the trailhead.

18 Bethel Spring

The newest of the Land Trust of North Alabama's preserves offers up a rugged, rocky hike to a stunning segmented-type waterfall formed by Bethel Spring. The wide, shimmering display tumbles down several courses toward its craggy rock base.

Height of falls: 75 feet
Type of falls: Segmented
Distance: 2.0-mile double loop
Difficulty: Moderate
Hiking time: About 1.5 hours
Start: At the trailhead kiosk on the northeast side of the parking lot
Trail surface: Rock, dirt
Best seasons: Sept–June; open 7 a.m.–7 p.m.
Canine compatibility: Dogs permitted; leash required
Fees and permits: None, donation requested
County: Madison

Land status: Land Trust of North Alabama preserve
Trail contact: Land Trust of North Alabama, 2442 Bankhead Pkwy. NE, Huntsville, AL 35801; (256) 534-5263; www.landtrustnal.org
Maps: *DeLorme: Alabama Atlas & Gazetteer.* Page 19, F10; additional trail maps available on the land trust's website
Special considerations: Doing the double loop counterclockwise as described in the Miles and Directions is easier than doing it in the opposite direction.

Finding the trailhead: From Huntsville, at the intersection of Old Highway 431 and US 431/ Governors Drive SW, take US 431 south 3.2 miles and turn left onto Old Highway 431. Travel 2 miles and turn left onto Cherry Tree Road. Drive 6 miles; the parking lot—with plenty of room for 20 cars—will be on the left. The trailhead is at a wooden rail fence and metal cattle gate on the northeast side of the parking lot. The trail starts here as a gravel road to the east. Trailhead GPS: N34 36.656' / W86 21.754'; Falls GPS: N34 37.091' / W86 21.958'

The Hike

The Land Trust of North Alabama has a mission—to preserve as much of the incredible landscapes and biodiversity of the Huntsville area as possible, creating greenspaces around the burgeoning city and, in turn, opening these properties for public use. They have done quite a job, protecting over 7,500 acres of land, more than 15 miles of creek and river frontage, and over fifty caves. Their latest preserve, as of this writing, is called Bethel Spring.

The centerpiece of this preserve is the spectacular cascade formed by the spring at the northernmost end of the preserve. The wide limestone walls channel several flows, creating a dazzling water show that flows into a 334-foot-deep cave known as Paul's Cave.

The hike to the falls uses four trails: Bethel Spring Loop, Carpenter, Falling Sink, and Mill. The trails are well marked with white diamond markers that have the name

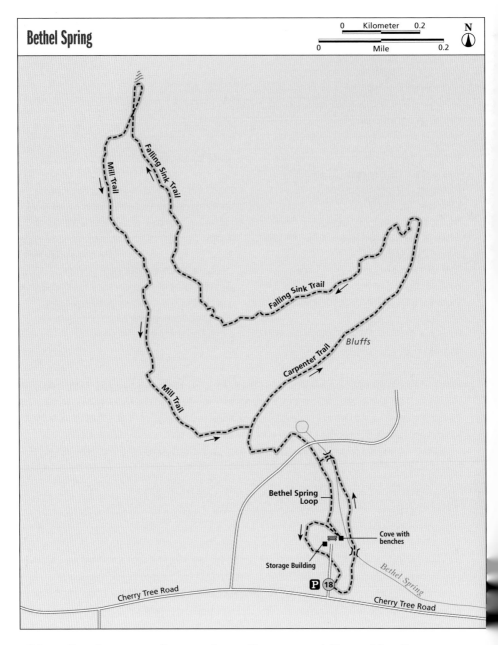

0 Kilometer 0.2

0 Mile 0.2

N

Mill Trail

Falling Sink Trail

Falling Sink Trail

Carpenter Trail

Bluffs

Mill Trail

Bethel Spring Loop

Cove with benches

Storage Building

P 18

Bethel Spring

Cherry Tree Road

Cherry Tree Road

of the trail you're on, as well as round, metallic-green medallions with yellow arrows pointing out the direction of turns.

We start the hike by hiking the double loop in a counterclockwise direction. It seems to be the easier way to go for most people. Starting out on the Bethel Spring Loop, the path is an 8- to 10-foot-wide, level gravel path. The trail parallels its namesake creek with its cool, clear water and soothing babbling sounds. To your right (east), there are expansive views of pasture grass and the surrounding mountains.

The waterfall at the Bethel Spring Preserve is a spectacular segmented falls that glides down its rocky face into a deep cave.

As you cross a second bridge over the spring, you come to the northern end of the first loop. Turn to the right (north) to head off the gravel path and start the Carpenter Trail. From here the trail becomes rockier, with a thick canopy to protect you from summer sun, until it meets up with the Falling Sink Trail, an extremely rocky, boulder-strewn path with a series of switchbacks up the hillside that passes alongside impressive bluffs culminating at the waterfall.

After exploring around the falls, you will pick up the Mill Trail to begin the trip back to the trailhead at the end of the Falling Sink Trail. This intersection can be a bit deceiving, as it begins right at the end of Falling Sink as a sharp left switchback near the falls. Hike south to close the big loop and head for the trailhead.

Miles and Directions

0.0 Start at the trailhead of the gravel Bethel Spring Loop to the east. In 300 feet cross the spring over a bridge.

0.2 After crossing a second bridge, turn right onto the Carpenter Trail.

0.3 Pass the Mill Trail on the left.

0.5 Pass below impressive bluffs.

0.6 The Falling Sink Trail begins at a sharp switchback to the left.

1.2 Arrive at the falls. After exploring, begin the trip back on the Mill Trail, which starts as a sharp switchback to the south at the end of the Falling Sink Trail.

1.6 The Mill Trail ends at the Carpenter Trail. Turn right (south) onto the Carpenter Trail.

1.8 Arrive back at the Bethel Spring Loop. Continue straight to the south.

1.9 Pass a storage house on the left.

2.0 Arrive back at the trailhead.

19 Alum Hollow

The Land Trust of North Alabama gives us yet another wonderful meandering hike along the ridges of Huntsville for views of the surrounding mountains and valleys, a visit to a deep rock shelter where Native Americans once lived over 10,000 years ago, and, of course, a waterfall—the gorgeous 30-foot tiered cascade—Alum Hollow Falls.

Height of falls: 30 feet
Type of falls: Tiered cascade
Distance: 2.3 miles out and back
Difficulty: Easy
Hiking time: About 1.5 hours
Start: On the south side of the Green Mountain Nature Preserve parking lot at the kiosk
Trail surface: Dirt and rock footpath
Best seasons: Sept–June; open sunrise–sunset
Canine compatibility: Dogs permitted; leash required

Fees and permits: None, donation requested
County: Madison
Land status: Nature preserve
Trail contact: Land Trust of North Alabama, 2707 Artie St. SW, Ste. 6, Huntsville, AL 35805; (256) 534-5263; www.landtrustnal.org
Maps: *DeLorme: Alabama Atlas & Gazetteer.* Page 19, F8; additional trail maps available on the land trust's website
Special considerations: Watch for trail runners and mountain bikes.

Finding the trailhead: From Huntsville, at the intersection of US 231 and Holmes Avenue SW, take US 231 south 5.6 miles and exit onto Memorial Parkway South. Travel 0.4 mile and turn left onto Haysland Road/Weatherly Road SE. Drive 1.5 miles and turn right onto Bailey Cove Road SE. Travel 1.5 miles and turn left onto Green Mountain Road SE. Drive 1.8 miles and turn right onto South Shawdee Road SE. In 2 miles, the well-marked parking lot will be on the right. The gravel lot has room for at least 20 cars. The trail begins on the south side of the parking lot at the kiosk. Trailhead GPS: N34 35.378' / W86 30.595'; Falls GPS: N34 35.469' / W86 31.247'

The Hike

This hike to Alum Hollow and its waterfall is perfect for hikers of all stripes and ages. Located in the Land Trust of North Alabama's (LTNA) Green Mountain Preserve, the hike is an easy walk along a ridge before making a short downhill climb to see the falls firsthand. The trail is wide, averaging 4 to 5 feet in width in some areas, with a tread that is a combination of sand, clay, dirt, and rock.

Throughout the hike there is a good canopy giving you protection from the summer sun. Flowering dogwoods along the trail accent the lush greens of summer, while the leaves of winged elm give way to brilliant yellow colors in the fall.

As with all LTNA trails, this one is well marked using white diamond markers with the LTNA logo on them and the name of the trail that you are on.

You will cross a couple of creeks along the route on footbridges, then at mile 0.8 you will hear the sound of a cascade down below the ridge to your left. This is not the Alum Hollow waterfall but another smaller cascade on the same creek that creates the falls that we will be visiting. As of this writing, there wasn't a trail down to this cascade. See hike 20, Talus Falls, for more.

Just a few yards past our turn downhill to visit Alum Hollow Falls, you will have a chance to visit Alum Cave. The cave is a deep rock shelter that was carved by the elements thousands of years ago. The limestone that fell from the rock face (known as chert) was later used by Native Americans of the Middle Woodland Period (between 200 BC and AD 300) for weapons, with the rock shelter protecting them from the elements. Remember, as with all historic sites, artifacts found in this area are protected. If you find any, do not remove them.

While this is an easy hike, the well-groomed trails are shared with mountain bikers and trail runners, so be aware and on the lookout as you round bends. If you want a hike that's a little more difficult and challenging, there is an option just for you (see Miles and Directions).

The waterfall at Alum Hollow slides down into a narrow bowl and pool.

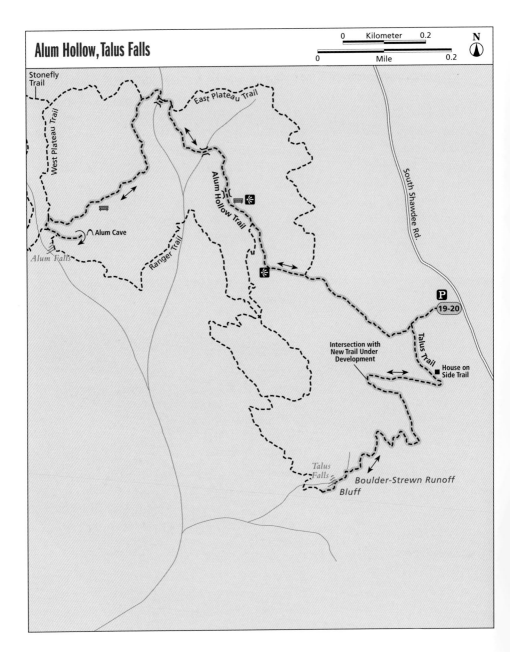

Stonefly Trail

West Plateau Trail

East Plateau Trail

Alum Hollow Trail

Ranger Trail

Alum Cave

Alum Falls

South Shawdee Rd.

P 19-20

Talus Trail

Intersection with New Trail Under Development

House on Side Trail

Talus Falls

Boulder-Strewn Runoff Bluff

The volunteers who help maintain the trails on LTNA properties do an amazing job. There is a donation kiosk at the trailhead. Please consider dropping in a few dollars to help them continue their mission and keep all the trails open for public use.

Miles and Directions

0.0 Begin on the south end of the parking lot at the kiosk. The trail heads off from here to the west. In 400 feet, the trail Ys, with the Talus Trail (hike 20) taking the left fork. Take the right fork onto the Alum Hollow Trail.

0.3 Pass the East Plateau Trail on the right. In less than 0.1 mile there is a bluff with a view of the surrounding hills in winter.

0.4 Pass the Ranger Trail on the left. In less than 0.1 mile, pass a bench at an overlook with a view in winter.

0.5 Cross a creek over a 20-foot bridge. In less than 0.1 mile, cross another creek over a 15-foot bridge.

0.7 Where the opposite end of the East Plateau Trail comes in on the right, take the left fork. In less than 0.1 mile, cross another creek over a 20-foot bridge. The trail begins to switchback briefly uphill as you pass the Nature's Ridge Trail on the right and then the West Plateau Trail.

0.9 Pass a bench on the left.

1.0 Pass the opposite end of the West Plateau Trail on the right.

1.1 Get your first view of the falls as you pass the Stonefly Trail on the right. The Alum Hollow Trail ends here and the Ranger Trail continues straight to the south. Continue straight on the Ranger Trail a few yards to view Alum Cave. When ready, turn around to this point and head steeply downhill toward the creek.

1.2 Arrive at Alum Falls. When ready, turn around and retrace your steps to the trailhead.

2.3 Arrive back at the trailhead.

Option: If you want a more challenging hike, make this into a 2.2-mile lollipop loop. After visiting the waterfall at mile 1.2, you can pick up the difficult and rugged 0.6-mile-long Ranger Trail and follow it back to where it meets up with the Alum Hollow Trail at mile 0.4.

20 Talus Falls

You will get a good cardio workout on this difficult, boulder-strewn hike to see Talus Falls. Located in the Land Trust of North Alabama's Green Mountain Preserve, Talus is quite different from any other waterfall we've seen so far. This small cascade pours out of the rock at the base of a tall limestone wall and makes you think it's a towering rush of water when in reality it's only a few feet tall.

See map on page 74.
Height of falls: 5 feet
Type of falls: Cascade
Distance: 1.2 miles out and back
Difficulty: Difficult
Hiking time: About 1 hour
Start: On the south side of the Green Mountain Nature Preserve parking lot at the kiosk
Trail surface: Dirt and rock footpath, boulder-strewn creek bed
Best seasons: Fall–spring; open sunrise–sunset

Canine compatibility: Dogs permitted; leash required
Fees and permits: None, donation requested
County: Madison
Land status: Nature preserve
Trail contact: Land Trust of North Alabama, 2707 Artie St. SW, Ste. 6, Huntsville, AL 35805; (256) 534-5263; www.landtrustnal.org
Maps: *DeLorme: Alabama Atlas & Gazetteer:* Page 19, F8; additional trail maps available on the land trust's website
Special considerations: Watch for trail runners.

Finding the trailhead: From Huntsville, at the intersection of US 231 and Holmes Avenue SW, take US 231 south 5.6 miles and exit onto Memorial Parkway South. Travel 0.4 mile and turn left onto Haysland Road/Weatherly Road SE. Drive 1.5 miles and turn right onto Bailey Cove Road SE. Travel 1.5 miles and turn left onto Green Mountain Road SE. Drive 1.8 miles and turn right onto South Shawdee Road SE. In 2 miles, the well-marked parking lot will be on the right. The gravel lot has room for at least 20 cars. The trail begins on the south side of the parking lot at the kiosk. Trailhead GPS: N34 35.378' / W86 30.595'; Falls GPS: N34 35.139' / W86 30.752'

The Hike

This hike to Talus Falls is a fooler in more ways than one. The first deception is the falls itself. The waterfall is only about 5 feet tall or so, but what makes it unique is its sound. As you approach the towering rock amphitheater where the fall is located, you hear this roaring sound. Must be a huge waterfall, right? Wrong! The acoustics in this bowl amplify the sound of this little cascade, making you think it's much bigger.

But the waterfall is still unique in that it is completely underground, coursing through a rocky channel within that tall rock wall until it finally appears at the base.

Then there is the hike itself. In geologic terms, talus means "an outward sloping and accumulated heap or mass of rock fragments," an appropriate name for this trail if ever there was one.

The unique Talus Falls will fool you as you approach. The bowl canyon makes you think there is a thundering waterfall, but where is it? PHOTO COURTESY KATEY DEASEY, LTNA

As you head out on the Alum Hollow Trail (hike 19) then branch off onto the Talus Trail, you will pass a sign warning that the trail is rated difficult and should only be hiked by "experienced hikers." You'll wonder where they got that idea as you stroll the easy walking path through the tall grass of the hardwood forest. But then things change.

At mile 0.2 you begin heading steeply downhill. And it keeps on going, a drop of over 300 feet in less than a half mile, until it levels off for a just a bit before you have to do some gymnastics, clambering over large boulders as you continue downhill and then hike up to the base of the wall and the waterfall. For those of you who aren't prepared, it will be a workout.

The trail is marked with the white diamond LTNA markers bearing the trail name, as well as a few round, metallic-green discs with arrows pointing directions.

I mentioned in hike 19 (Alum Hollow Falls) that at one point you hear the sound of a cascade downhill from that trail, but there is no way down. LTNA tells me that they have begun building a new trail that will split off the Talus Trail at mile 0.3 and should lead to that cascade. Hopefully it will be ready by the time you read this.

Miles and Directions

0.0 Start from the trailhead at the kiosk on the south side of the parking lot on the Alum Hollow Trail. In less than 0.1 mile, come to a Y intersection. Take the left fork to begin the Talus Trail. A sign here warns that the path is difficult and for experienced hikers only.

0.1 Pass a house at the end of a side trail on the left.

0.2 The path becomes rockier as it begins a steady downhill.

0.3 At the bottom of the hill, come to an intersection. A new trail under development (as of this writing) heads to the right. Turn left (southeast) to continue on the Talus Trail.

0.5 The trail begins its steepest descent.

0.6 Clamber over large boulders in a runoff. In less than 0.1 mile, you will hear what sounds like a huge waterfall. Take the rocky side trail to the left, to the base of a tall rock bluff. Talus Falls is tucked away at the base. When ready, turn around and retrace your steps to the trailhead. (**Note:** If you reach the Talus Connector Trail, you've passed the side trail to the falls.)

1.2 Arrive back at the trailhead.

21 Neversink Pit

Get ready for another breathtaking visit to a deep karst sinkhole. Neversink Pit is a vertical drop of 162 feet with a stunning ribbon waterfall flowing into the abyss. The view is especially striking in spring and early summer with dark greenery and blooming mountain laurel framing the scene.

Height of falls: 162 feet
Type of falls: Cascade
Distance: 1.0 mile out and back
Difficulty: Difficult
Hiking time: About 1 hour
Start: At the trailhead on the east side of the parking area
Trail surface: Rock, dirt
Best seasons: Sept–June; open sunrise–sunset
Canine compatibility: Dogs permitted; leash required
Fees and permits: No fee; surface permit required (see text)
County: Jackson
Land status: Southeastern Cave Conservancy property

Trail contact: Southeastern Cave Conservancy, Inc., PO Box 250, Signal Mountain, TN 37377; (423) 771-9671; www.saveyourcaves.org; permits can be applied for online at https:// permits.scci.org
Maps: *DeLorme: Alabama Atlas & Gazetteer:* Page 20, C3; additional trail maps available when you request your permit
Special considerations: Neversink is extremely dangerous. It is a 162-foot plummet if you go off the edge. Do not attempt climbing down into it. Respect the edge of the rim by keeping a safe distance away. Cell phone service is questionable if you need help. Your permit is for surface hiking only unless you apply and are granted a special climbing permit.

Finding the trailhead: From Scottsboro, at the intersection of AL 35/Veterans Drive and AL 2, take AL 35/Veterans Drive 7.7 miles (along the route the highway becomes CR 21/Tupelo Pike then CR 470). Turn left onto CR 33 and travel 2.3 miles. Turn right onto CR 32. In 1.3 miles continue straight on CR 264. The small gravel parking lot—which is big enough for maybe 5 cars—is on the right tucked away in the woods. The trail begins on the east side of the parking lot. Trailhead GPS: N34 48.018' / W86 00.508'; Falls GPS: N34 48.284' / W86 00.305'

The Hike

There are some words that cannot be overused when it comes to describing the waterfalls of Alabama—stunning, breathtaking, incredible. *All* of those words perfectly describe our visit to the second sinkhole on our journey, Neversink Pit.

Neversink Pit is a 162-foot vertical-drop waterfall into a circular cave. The sinkhole was created by what is known as karst geology, a process where surface water erodes the soft limestone underground, forming an intricate series of underground passages and deep holes.

You may have seen photos of cavers silhouetted against the brilliant sunlit opening of the cave as they rappel to the bottom. Well, we're not going to the bottom, and

A stunning sight—the ribbon of water that flows into the 162-foot-deep sinkhole known as Neversink Pit.

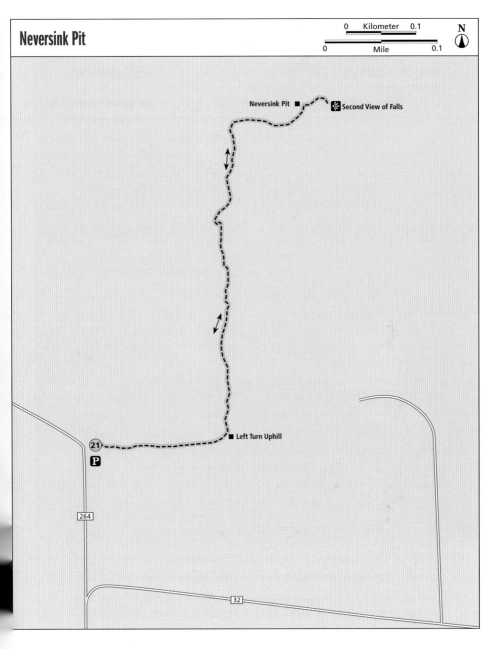

Neversink Pit ■

◈ Second View of Falls

■ Left Turn Uphill

㉑

Ⓟ

264

32

don't even think about it (more in a moment). We're here for the stunning waterfall that cascades down the pit's rocky walls.

Neversink is owned and managed by the Southeastern Cave Conservancy, Inc. (SCCI). The conservancy not only protects sensitive cave habitats and wildlife but also opens the property up to the public for recreational activity including hiking to the falls.

To hike Neversink, you must have what SCCI calls a "surface permit," which means no climbing down into the sinkhole. The permit is free and available online by visiting the permit website (see Trail contact). Simply register your name, complete the form, and in minutes you will have your permit. The only restriction for obtaining a permit is the number of people who are allowed in the preserve on any given day.

Once you have been approved, read the permit carefully and be sure to follow all the rules. Print out two copies of the permit—one to carry with you and one to put on the dashboard of your vehicle. When you apply for that permit, you may want to consider making a donation to SCCI to help them continue their mission.

Begin the hike on the east side of the parking lot at the kiosk. Be aware that for much of the trip, private property is not far from either side of the trail. Please respect the property owners and stay on the trail and SCCI land.

The trail is marked with yellow plastic diamond markers adorned with the SCCI logo, as well as blue flagging tape that says "SCCI."

The first 0.1 mile is a nice easy walk next to a pasture with cows and views of the surrounding mountains to your right, but soon the path narrows and swings to the north and becomes very rocky with small boulders and rock jumbles to navigate around and over. Just remember to keep your eyes up and look for those markers. It's easy to set off on a game trail.

The entire hike has a good canopy that provides needed cover from the hot southern sun. Some of the level areas of the trail where it is mainly dirt can retain water after a good rain and become thick with mud.

Finally, 0.5 mile from the trailhead you arrive at the rim and get your first view of the falls. If you turn right (east) here, a small trail takes you to a bluff where you can get a view from a different angle, but please, it is very steep and can be slippery, so stay a safe distance away from the edge.

When ready, turn around and retrace your steps to the trailhead.

Miles and Directions

0.0 Start at the kiosk on the east side of the parking lot.

0.1 The trail makes a sharp left away from a pasture and begins to head steeply uphill.

0.5 Arrive at your first view of the falls. Remember, it is a very dangerous bluff. Stay clear of the edge. When ready, turn right (east) and in less than 0.1 mile, get a second view of the falls. When ready, retrace your steps to the trailhead.

1.0 Arrive back at the trailhead.

22 Pisgah Gorge

Hidden away on the backroads of the tiny town of Pisgah, you will find this easy hike to view an impressive pair of sparkling, cascading waterfalls formed by Little Bryant Creek, plus get a wonderful sweeping view of the gorge they helped form. The first 0.3 mile of this hike is ADA accessible.

Height of falls: 100 feet each
Type of falls: Cascade
Distance: 1.1 miles out and back (T-shaped)
Difficulty: Easy; first 0.3 mile is ADA accessible
Hiking time: About 30 minutes
Start: At the entrance to Pisgah Civitan Park at the steel gate and gravel road
Trail surface: Partial gravel and cement path, then dirt and rock
Best seasons: Year-round; open 10 a.m.–6 p.m.
Canine compatibility: Dogs permitted; leash required

Fees and permits: None
County: Jackson
Land status: City park
Trail contact: Town of Pisgah, Alabama, PO Box 2, Pisgah, AL 35765; (256) 451-3232; www.townofpisgah.com
Maps: DeLorme: Alabama Atlas & Gazetteer. Page 20, E5
Special considerations: Part of this hike takes you to the top of the falls at an old cement dam. Do not walk on the dam. The view of the second falls on a bluff has a precipitous and dangerous drop. Use caution.

Finding the trailhead: From Scottsboro, at the intersection of AL 35/Veterans Drive and US 72, take AL 35/Veterans Drive 3.2 miles and turn left onto AL 40 East. Travel 6.9 miles and make a slight left onto AL 71 North. Drive 2.4 miles and turn left onto CR 58. Travel 2.2 miles and turn left onto CR 374. The Pisgah Civitan Park will be ahead on the left in 0.6 mile. The hike directions described here begin at the park entrance if the gate to the park is closed, which it often is. Trailhead GPS: N34 40.506' / W85 51.512'; Falls GPS: N34 40.339' / W85 51.391'

The Hike

This hike to the twin falls of Pisgah Gorge is an easy walk that combines a short section of gravel, cement, and pavement walk with a relatively easy narrow dirt and rock footpath. The first 0.3 mile are a gravel and cement path, which makes it easy for those with disabilities to view the upper falls.

The hike begins at the main entrance to the Pisgah Civitan Park. Unless there is a baseball game or other event going on when you arrive, the gate is normally closed. Park off to the side of the gate so you don't block the entrance and walk around it to the southwest on the gravel road. When you arrive at the Civitan picnic pavilion and stage, the path becomes cement. Continue to follow it to the south and you'll arrive at a large wooden amphitheater where you get a view of the upper falls. This section from the parking area to the amphitheater is ADA accessible. The remainder of the hike is not.

An easy walk that is partially ADA accessible leads you through a city park to the spectacular Pisgah Gorge waterfall.

From this vantage point you will notice that there is a small dam at the top of the falls. At one time an old mill was located there, but these waterfalls were here a long time before the mill, as is evidenced by the deep canyon that they forged over the centuries.

But the trip isn't over yet. From here, a narrow dirt and rock footpath splits off to the east and west to follow the rim of the gorge. The trail to the east is a beautiful walk in the woods in spring and summer with an incredible amount of pink and white mountain laurel blooming, forming a visually stunning frame around the trail.

You'll get to view the second or lower falls at mile 0.5 from atop an open, rocky bluff. You will also have a wonderful view of the gorge itself, which is reminiscent (although on a much, much smaller scale) of Little River Canyon (hikes 28 and 29).

From here, you will turn around and head back to the amphitheater, but don't head to your car yet. Instead, continue straight to the west and you will come to the top of the upper falls and an old dam. You'll have a nice view down the gorge from here, but don't walk on the dam.

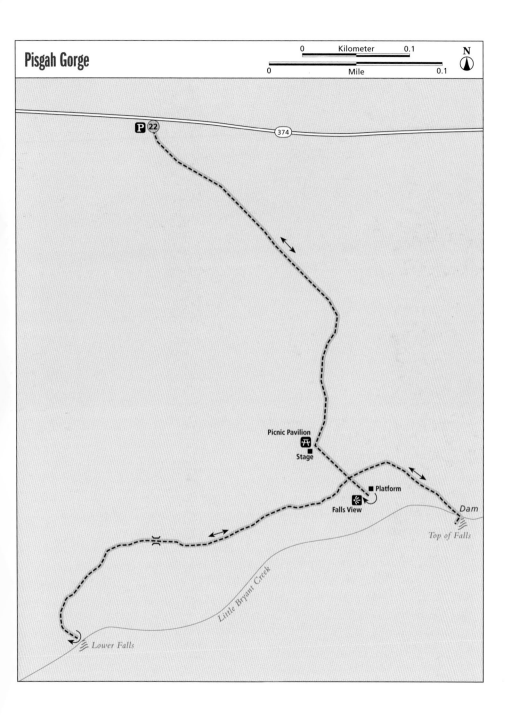

Pisgah Gorge

This picture really doesn't do the trail justice as you walk through tunnels of mountain laurel.

Miles and Directions

0.0 Start at the parking area, walking around the park gate, and head south on the gravel road.

0.2 Pass the Pisgah Civitan picnic pavilion and stage on the right. Pick up a cement sidewalk here and continue south.

0.3 A trail crosses your path. We'll return here in a minute, but right now, continue straight and in less than 0.1 mile, arrive at the viewing platform and the falls. When ready, retrace your steps to the intersection and turn left onto the dirt path.

0.4 Cross a short footbridge.

0.5 Turn left (south) and in less than 0.1 mile, get a view of the lower falls. Use caution on the bluff. When ready, retrace your steps to the intersection at mile 0.3.

0.7 Back at the intersection, continue straight to the east.

0.8 Arrive at the top of the falls and dam. When ready, retrace your steps to the trailhead.

1.1 Arrive back at the trailhead.

23 DeSoto Falls

One of the tallest, most stunning, and most visited waterfalls in Alabama, DeSoto Falls was once a natural waterfall, but in 1925 the West Fork of Little River was dammed to create the state's first hydroelectric plant. From the dam, the torrent thunders down a second rocky tier before crashing to a beautiful pool below. There is a second way to visit the falls for those with small children or physical disabilities (see hike 24, DeSoto Falls Picnic Area).

Height of falls: 104 feet
Type of falls: Tiered plunge
Distance: 2.0 miles out and back (V-shaped)
Difficulty: Moderate
Hiking time: About 1 hour
Start: At the pull-off on CR 613 to the south
Trail surface: Rocks, boulders
Best seasons: Year-round; open sunrise–sunset
Canine compatibility: Dogs permitted; leash required

Fees and permits: None
County: DeKalb
Land status: State park
Trail contact: DeSoto State Park, 7104 DeSoto Pkwy. NE, Fort Payne, AL 35967; (256) 845-0051; www.alapark.com/parks/desoto-state-park
Maps: *DeLorme: Alabama Atlas & Gazetteer:* Page 21, G8
Special considerations: While year-round, the falls can still slow considerably in the summer.

Finding the trailhead: From Mentone, at the intersection of AL 117 and CR 89, take AL 117 south 1.3 miles. Turn right onto Tutwiler Gap and travel 1.1 miles. Turn left onto CR 613. Travel 0.6 mile. The parking area is a narrow dirt pull-off on the right side of the road with enough room for 10 to 15 cars. It's best to pull straight in, leaving room for others. Trailhead GPS: N34 33.104' / W85 35.765'; Falls GPS: N34 32.938' / W85 35.520'

The Hike

This hike uses two unnamed, un-blazed trails (that is, as of this writing—more in a moment) that lead to views of DeSoto Falls. The upper trail takes you to a great view of the falls from the top of the canyon rim, while the lower trail takes you to the canyon floor and breathtaking views of the torrent from water level, complete with a little of its spray as a bonus.

It doesn't matter which trail you take first. The two join at the trailhead, making a V shape, so you can either do the full hike as I describe here or separate the hikes into two out-and-back routes.

I mentioned that these trails are unnamed and un-blazed as of this writing. That will most likely change by the time you read this. The trails along the rim and through the canyon itself used to be on private property, but the state's Forever Wild program has purchased the land, and the trails will become official DeSoto State Park trails very soon.

The 104-foot tiered DeSoto Falls is one of the tallest in the state.

The upper trail takes the left fork of the V and is an easy walking trek over a well-worn dirt and rock footpath. Along the way, you will cross a spring that is the top of a second, smaller but seasonal waterfall. You will have a chance to see the full waterfall from its base on the second half of the hike on the lower trail. The turnaround for this portion of the hike is atop a large rock outcropping at mile 0.4 where you'll get a spectacular panoramic view of DeSoto Falls.

Turn around here and head back to the trailhead, where you will hike a few yards past the parking area to the west down a powerline. At the bottom of the hill, turn to the left (south) and you will pick up the second well-worn path.

The lower trail follows the base of a tall bluff line and scampers between large boulders. You will visit an impressive rock shelter called the Ice Box along the way. Soon you will arrive at a sandy beach with an amazing view of the river's turbulent turquoise water.

At this point, the trail is hard to make out, but it turns to the left (southeast) where you will encounter one rock scramble after another all the way to the turnaround and a breathtaking view of the falls from a rock slab along the banks of the river. As you walk this section, be on the lookout for remnants of the old power plant, including metal cogs and steel braces.

DeSoto Falls, DeSoto Falls Picnic Area

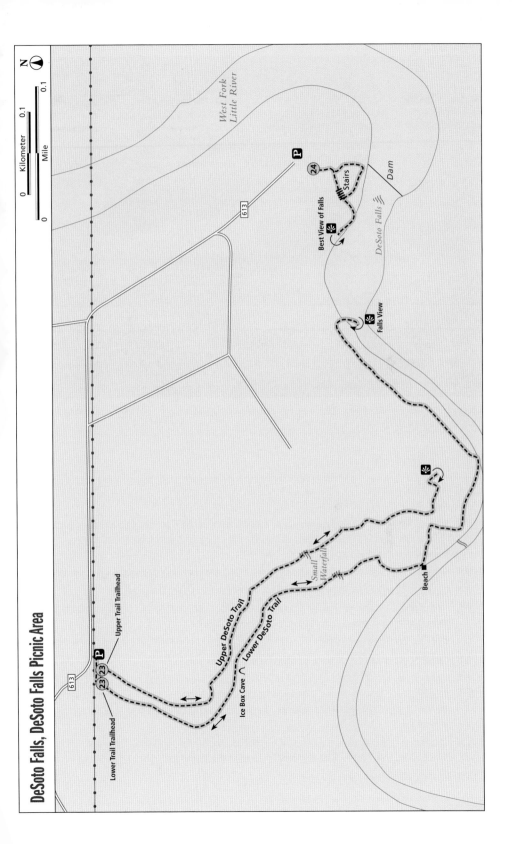

On your way to DeSoto Falls, you'll get up close and personal with the boiling waters of the West Fork of Little River.

Miles and Directions

0.0   Start at the trailhead located on the west side of the parking pull-off. Head south on the worn path into the woods.

0.3   Cross a seasonal stream and the top of a small waterfall. We'll see the full falls at mile 1.0. In less than 0.1 mile, the path is hugging the base of a tall rock bluff. Get your first view of the falls in winter.

0.4   View the falls from a rock outcropping. Turn around and retrace your steps to the trailhead.

0.7   At the trailhead, turn left (west) and follow the powerline a short distance.

0.8   At the bottom of the hill, turn left (south) to begin the lower trail. In less than 0.1 mile, walk through a split rock.

0.9   Pass Ice Box Cave on the left.

1.0   Arrive at the base of the small, seasonal waterfall from mile 0.3.

1.1   Arrive at the bottom of the canyon at the river. There is a small, sandy beach here. It's hard to see but the trail continues over some large rocks to the southeast. In less than 0.1 mile, there is a short side trail where you can view some rapids. The trail is now nonstop rock scrambles.

1.4   Climb over a large rock and arrive at a big, flat rock slab and the ultimate view of the falls. When ready, turn around and retrace your steps to the trailhead.

2.0   Arrive back at the trailhead.

24 DeSoto Falls Picnic Area

Another way to view the spectacular DeSoto Falls without a rugged hike down into the canyon is by visiting the DeSoto Falls Picnic Area, located next to the A.A. Miller Dam, which feeds the tiered 104-foot waterfall. The overlook provides incredible views of the falls and canyon from the top of the turbulent cascade, and is plenty safe for youngsters plus affords people with disabilities and special needs a chance to safely view the falls. Just remember to stay behind the railing even when the falls runs slow in the late summer. It is tempting to walk out on the rocks, but don't.

See map on page 89.
Height of falls: 104 feet
Type of falls: Tiered plunge
Distance: 0.2-mile meander
Difficulty: Easy
Hiking time: About 30 minutes
Start: At the kiosk on the south side of the parking lot
Trail surface: Natural stone and cement path
Best seasons: Year-round; open sunrise–sunset
Canine compatibility: Dogs permitted; leash required

Fees and permits: Parking fee
County: Dekalb
Land status: State park
Trail contact: DeSoto State Park, 7104 DeSoto Pkwy. NE, Fort Payne, AL 35967; (256) 845-0051; www.alapark.com/parks/desoto-state-park
Maps: *DeLorme: Alabama Atlas & Gazetteer.* Page 21, G8
Special considerations: While year-round, the falls can still slow considerably in the summer. Stay behind the railing.

Finding the trailhead: From Mentone, at the intersection of AL 117 and CR 89, take AL 117 west 1.3 miles. Turn left onto Tutwiler Gap and travel 1.1 miles. Turn left onto CR 613. Travel 0.7 mile and CR 613 becomes DeSoto Falls Road. Continue an additional 0.3 mile; the parking lot will be on the right. There are men's and women's restrooms available. Trailhead GPS: N34 32.962' / W85 35.403'; Falls GPS: N34 32.950' / W85 35.451'

The Hike

This hike is actually more of a meander around the overlook high above the canyon that is formed by the West Fork of Little River and the action of DeSoto Falls. The picnic area has plenty of parking and picnic tables as well as large, clean restrooms.

There really isn't a right or wrong way to walk the rim to see the falls. The trip begins from the south side of the parking lot at the kiosk. From there, simply stroll down the cement walkway where you will come to a Y intersection. Straight ahead takes you up close and personal with the top of the falls and the A.A. Miller Dam that once powered the region's first hydroelectric plant. The right fork takes you to a set of stairs with inlaid quotes by John Muir.

After furnishing electric power to two other southern towns, Arthur Abernathy Miller, a self-educated electrical engineer, set his sights on supplying power to Fort Payne. His goal was to build a dam across the West Fork of Little River at DeSoto Falls. The original dam was 10 feet tall, then later increased to 20 feet. At first, the company he founded, Little River Power Company, only allowed the electricity to flow from sunset to midnight, but after many women in the town began purchasing more electric irons, he allowed the town to be powered an additional hour or two on Thursday afternoons so they could complete the ironing, eventually letting it flow all day seven days a week. It's interesting to note that there wasn't a main switch to turn the streetlights on and off. A young man named Ernest Wallis would ride up and down the streets of Fort Payne manually turning the streetlights on, then return later to turn them off, one of the last "lamp lighters," only in a modern age.

The walkway around the rim is flat, natural stone but still a bit uneven, so watch your step. The path to the right of the stairs becomes narrow and at this point may not be suitable for people with disabilities. Use your best judgment.

◀ *Top: Getting a bird's-eye view of one of the state's tallest waterfalls from the top—DeSoto Falls.*
Bottom: A couple marvels at the dam that forms the famous DeSoto Falls.

25 Azalea Cascade, Laurel and Lost Falls Loop

One of the highlights of a visit to DeSoto State Park is a 2.4-mile loop hike to three of the park's many falls—Azalea Cascade, Laurel Falls, and Lost Falls. This hike is perfect for families with its relatively level walking. Lost and Laurel Falls are inset off the main trail in beautiful and secluded niches. You will get your feet wet as you cross the top of Lost Falls. Azalea Cascade lives up to its name in spring and summer when it is framed by colorful azaleas and mountain laurel.

Height of falls: Azalea Cascade, 6 feet; Laurel Falls, 25 feet; Lost Falls, 20 feet
Type of falls: Azalea, cascade; Lost and Laurel, tiered cascade
Distance: 2.4-mile loop
Difficulty: Easy
Hiking time: About 1.5 hours
Start: At the Talmadge Butler Boardwalk Trail
Trail surface: Rock and dirt footpath, short boardwalk
Best seasons: Year-round; open sunrise-sunset; country store open 9 a.m.–5 p.m.

Canine compatibility: Dogs permitted; leash required
Fees and permits: None
County: DeKalb
Land status: State park
Trail contact: DeSoto State Park, 7104 DeSoto Pkwy. NE, Fort Payne, AL 35967; (256) 845-0051; www.alapark.com/parks/desoto-state-park
Maps: DeLorme: Alabama Atlas & Gazetteer: Page 21, G8; trail maps available at the park's camp store
Special considerations: None. Just have fun.

Finding the trailhead: From Mentone, at the intersection of AL 117 and CR 89, take AL 117 south 1.4 miles and turn right on East River Road/CR 177. Travel 0.4 mile and turn right onto CR 177/CR 630/Alpine Road and continue for 1.1 miles. Turn right onto CR 106. Travel 0.9 mile and CR 106 becomes Wester Road. Travel 3 miles and Wester Road becomes CR 165. Travel 0.6 mile and turn left onto Lookout Mountain Parkway. In 0.5 mile the Talmadge Butler Boardwalk will be on the left. There is room for about 15 cars here. Trailhead GPS: N34 29.939' / W85 37.070'; Falls GPS: Azalea Cascade, N34 29.837' / W85 37.175'; Laurel Falls, N34 29.724' / W85 37.462'; Lost Falls, N34 29.689' / W85 37.911'

The Hike

This loop through DeSoto State Park is a perfect introduction to the waterfalls of Alabama for beginners or anyone who wants a nice walk in the woods to relax next to the soothing sounds of a waterfall.

The dirt and rock footpath is not very difficult at all and is well blazed. We will be using four separate trails to complete the loop—the Talmadge Butler Boardwalk, the red-blazed Azalea Cascade Trail, the blue-blazed Laurel Falls Trail, and the orange-blazed Lost Falls Trail.

The hike begins on the composite Talmadge Butler Boardwalk. Along this section, you will pass several benches, picnic tables, and a picnic pavilion where you can sit next to the calming waters of the creek that forms the three falls. At the end of the boardwalk, you will be treated to the first waterfall, the sliding cascade of Azalea Cascade, which lives up to its name in spring and summer when it is framed with beautiful white and pink azaleas and mountain laurel.

Following the cascade, the trail can appear to be a bit jumbled. Continue straight off the boardwalk, passing an exit to the Azalea Cascade Trail, and cross the base of the cascade over a bridge. On the other side, the trail heads steeply up a short hill using railroad tie and dirt stairs. Soon after the top of the climb, you will cross the creek again over a bridge and then turn left, picking up the Azalea Cascade Trail on the

One of three waterfalls along a short loop within DeSoto State Park, Lost Falls puts on a spectacular water show.

opposite side. At mile 0.3 the trail Ys. Take the right fork to begin the Lost Falls Trail. From there, it is smooth sailing to the other two falls.

Laurel Falls is on a side trail off to the left of the main trail at mile 0.8. Be looking for a stone marker on the ground with the name of the falls etched in it at the turn.

From here all the way to Lost Falls, you will make several easy creek crossings. Some parts of the trail follow runoffs that make it slick after a good rain. Just take it slow and watch your step.

Another side trail leads to the base of Lost Falls at the northern end of the loop. When ready, clamber back up to the Lost Falls Trail and carefully cross the top of the falls over the flat stone. Once on the other side, you will pick up the blue-blazed Laurel Falls Trail for the trip back.

You may be able to see Laurel Falls once again on the return trip, but in summer the view is obscured with foliage.

As you head back to the trailhead, you will pass beneath some small rock outcroppings and visit some interesting shallow rock shelters.

This hike takes you across the top of Lost Falls.

Azalea Cascade, Laurel and Lost Falls Loop; Indian Falls; Lodge Falls

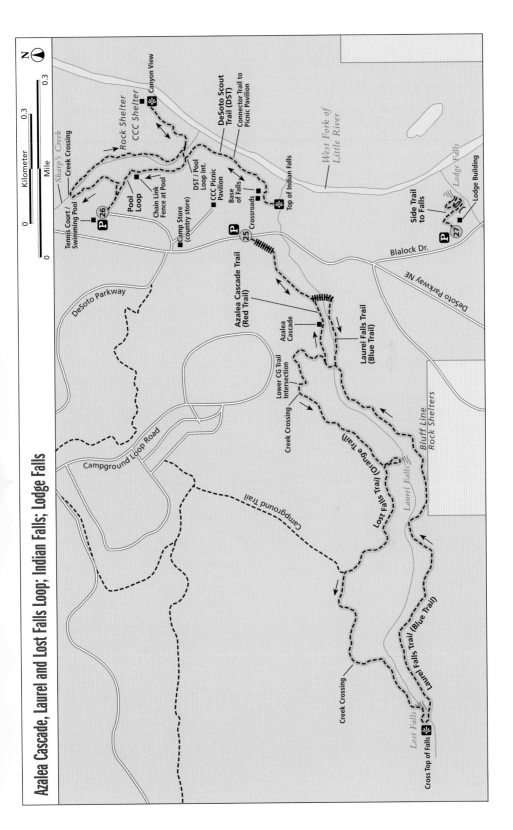

Miles and Directions

0.0 Start at the trailhead for the Talmadge Butler Boardwalk.

0.1 Pass a picnic pavilion on the left.

0.2 Continue straight (south), crossing a bridge for a view of Azalea Cascade. On the other side, the boardwalk ends. Climb a steep set of steps to the south. You are on the red-blazed Azalea Cascade Trail.

0.3 Cross a bridge to the north. On the other side, the trail splits to the north (straight) and east (right). Continue straight to the north on the red-blazed trail.

0.4 Pass through a split rock and, in a few feet, pick up the orange-blazed Lost Falls Trail.

0.5 Pass the Lower Campground Trail on the right. In less than 0.1 mile, cross a creek.

0.7 On the ground to the left you will see a stone with the words "Lost Falls" etched in it. Turn left (south) and head to the falls. In less than 0.1 mile, arrive at the base of the falls. When ready, turn around and retrace your steps to the Lost Falls Trail.

0.8 Back on the trail, turn left (west).

1.0 Pass the Campground Trail on the right. It is also blazed orange so don't be confused. Continue straight to the west.

1.2 Cross a 10-foot-wide creek over flat stone.

1.3 Turn left (southeast) onto an unmarked side trail and head to Lost Falls.

1.4 Arrive at the base of the falls. When ready, turn around and head uphill and turn left (west), walking a few yards to the top of the falls. Carefully cross the falls over the flat rock surface. Once across, turn left (south) and pick up the blue-blazed Laurel Falls Trail.

1.9 Pass Laurel Falls on the left.

2.0 A long rock bluff begins with a few small rock shelters here, including what used to be called "CC Caves."

2.2 Cross a creek over a bridge to the north. On the opposite side, turn right (east) onto the red-blazed Azalea Cascade Trail.

2.3 Get a view of the top of Azalea Cascade on the right. In less than 0.1 mile, rejoin the boardwalk and follow it to the trailhead.

2.4 Arrive back at the trailhead.

26 Indian Falls

A rugged 1.3-mile loop hike along the DeSoto Scout Trail (DST) presents you with views of the turbulent blue-green waters of the West Fork of Little River and a breathtaking view of the canyon formed by the river, all culminating in a visit to the 25-foot-tall cascade known as Indian Falls. The trail is moderate in difficulty with plenty of ups and downs. You can also join this hike with hike 27, Lodge Falls, to extend it to 2.1 miles (see the option in Miles and Directions).

See map on page 97.
Height of falls: 25 feet
Type of falls: Cascade
Distance: 1.3-mile narrow loop
Difficulty: Moderate
Hiking time: About 1 hour
Start: At the DeSoto State Park pool or tennis courts
Trail surface: Dirt and rock footpath
Best seasons: Year-round; open sunrise–sunset; country store open 9 a.m.–5 p.m.
Canine compatibility: Dogs permitted; leash required

Fees and permits: None
County: DeKalb
Land status: State park
Trail contact: DeSoto State Park, 7104 DeSoto Pkwy. NE, Fort Payne, AL 35967; (251) 845-0051; www.alapark.com/parks/desoto-state-park
Maps: *DeLorme: Alabama Atlas & Gazetteer.* Page 21, G8; trail maps available at the park's camp store
Special considerations: There are plenty of boulder scrambles along the riverbanks and a steep climb out of the canyon to the falls.

Finding the trailhead: From Fort Payne on I-59 at exit 218, head east on Glenn Boulevard SW/Pine Ridge Road SW 1 mile and turn left onto Gault Avenue South. Travel 1.1 miles and turn right onto 5th Street. Travel 0.4 mile and turn left onto Wallace Avenue NE. Follow Wallace Avenue NE 2 miles and turn left onto CR 89/DeSoto Parkway NE. Travel 5.7 miles. At the DeSoto State Park country store, turn right into the picnic area then make an immediate left. In 0.2 mile you will arrive at the tennis courts. If the gate to the pool parking lot is not closed, turn right here and park at the swimming pool building. If it is, park at the tennis courts. Trailhead GPS: N34 30.069' / W85 38.057'; Falls GPS: N34 29.910' / W85 37.000'

The Hike

While you could do a short 0.6-mile out-and-back hike to Indian Falls from DeSoto State Park's picnic area near the country store, this rugged loop gives you so much more to see.

We will be using a section of the 16-mile-long DeSoto Scout Trail (DST) plus the Pool Loop Trail and Cabin Trail to view the canyon that was formed by the West Fork of Little River thousands of years ago as well as the river's roaring rapids from high atop a rocky bluff, before dipping down for a riverside view of those rapids then once again head steeply back up the canyon to our destination, Indian Falls.

Indian Falls plummets down the rock wall at DeSoto State Park to feed the raging West Fork of Little River.

The trek is rated moderate, but with the climb out of the canyon and many rock scrambles along the river, some might find it difficult depending on their conditioning.

You will have a chance to see Indian Falls twice, once from its base and then from the top from a vantage point on a wooden footbridge that crosses the falls. There is usually a flow of water at the falls, but in the heat of summer during drought conditions, both the falls and river can dry up to a trickle.

The best time to see the real character of the West Fork and Indian Falls is to visit the park in late fall to late spring when the rains really kick it up. And, of course, fall provides a bonus splash of color as the hardwoods spring to life with amazing autumn colors. In spring and summer, the trail is lined with white and pink rhododendron, mountain laurel, and azaleas. The blossoms and their sweet fragrance linger in the air.

The trails are marked with paint blazes: blue for the Pool Loop, lime green for the Cabin Trail, and yellow for the DeSoto Scout Trail itself. You will also see a few yellow wooden signs with red lettering that read "DST."

Your hike begins at the state park's pool. In summer when the pool is open, you can park here in the large paved lot. Access is prohibited in the off-seasons, so instead park at the tennis courts, which are only a few dozen yards away. The blue Pool Loop Trail begins on the left side (north) of the pool's parking lot as you are looking at the pool.

Miles and Directions

0.0 Start from either the parking lot at the tennis courts or the pool house as noted in the text and Finding the Trailhead. Head toward the pool house; once there, head north toward the woods. Look for the brown sign with a hiker logo on it and duck into the woods on the blue-blazed Pool Loop. The path is thick with a tunnel of azaleas, rhododendron, and holly.

0.2 The trail appears to "Y." Straight ahead is a game trail. Turn to the right (northeast). Just after the turn cross a short bridge over Sharp's Creek.

0.3 The trail passes a nice cascade in the stream to the right (southwest) and heads downhill on wooden railroad tie steps.

0.4 Come to the intersection of the DeSoto Scout Trail and the Pool Loop. The blue trail continues off to the right (west.) Follow the yellow blazes of the DST to the left (east) for a short side trip to a view.

0.5 Arrive at a CCC trail shelter with an impressive view of the canyon and river below. Turn around here and head back to the Pool Loop/DeSoto Scout Trail intersection you passed at mile 0.4.

0.6 Back at the intersection, turn left (west) and head steeply downhill on the conjoined trails (the path is blazed both blue and yellow).

0.7 At the bottom of the hill cross a 20-foot bridge over Sharp's Creek. Following the bridge, the Pool Loop heads uphill to the right (northwest). Turn left to continue on the DST.

0.9 Come to a four-way intersection or crossroad. Go straight and in 200 feet arrive at the base of Indian Falls (watch your head on the low rock overhang). When ready, go back to the crossroad and turn left, climbing uphill using some stairs. At the top of the hill, turn left (west) onto the DST. In less than 0.1 mile view Indian Falls from a 50-foot-long bridge that crosses the top of the falls. When ready, turn around and retrace your steps or follow the Cabin Trail to mile 0.7.

1.1 Turn left onto the Pool Loop Trail. There is a steep drop to your right along this narrow trail.

1.2 Come to chain-link fence next to the pool building. Follow it around to the left (north) back to the pool parking lot.

1.3 Arrive back at the trailhead.

Option: To make this a 1.9-mile hike, at mile 0.9, turn left onto the Cabin Trail and cross the bridge over Indian Falls. In 0.3 mile, arrive at Lodge Falls (hike 27). After viewing, turn around and retrace your steps.

27 Lodge Falls

Another short but rugged hike at DeSoto State Park leads you to the aptly named Lodge Falls, so named because, well, it's behind the park's lodge. Average hikers won't have much trouble with the climb down and back up, but it may be too steep for some.

See map on page 97.
Height of falls: 25 feet
Type of falls: Cascade
Distance: 0.2 mile out and back
Difficulty: Moderate
Hiking time: About 15 minutes
Start: At the lodge parking lot on the right side of the building
Trail surface: Rock, dirt
Best seasons: Sept–June; open sunrise–sunset
Canine compatibility: Dogs permitted; leash required

Fees and permits: None
County: DeKalb
Land status: State park
Trail contact: DeSoto State Park, 7104 DeSoto Pkwy. NE, Fort Payne, AL 35967; (251) 845-0051; www.alapark.com/parks/ desoto-state-park
Maps: *DeLorme: Alabama Atlas & Gazetteer.* Page 21, G8; trail maps available at the park's camp store
Special considerations: It is a considerable climb down the hillside from the lodge.

Finding the trailhead: From Mentone, at the intersection of AL 117 and CR 89, take AL 117 east for 1.4 miles and turn right onto CR 177/CR 630. Travel 6.5 miles and turn right onto East River Road. Travel 0.4 mile and turn left onto Wester Road, then in a few feet turn right to continue on AL 177/CR 630 (Alpine Road) for another 1.1 miles. Turn right onto CR 106 and travel 4.5 miles (CR 106 is also named Wester Road, then becomes CR 165). Turn left onto Lookout Mountain Parkway and drive 0.3 mile, to where the parkway becomes DeSoto Parkway NE. Continue an additional 0.4 mile and turn left onto Blalock Drive. Drive 0.2 mile and the parking lot for the lodge will be on the left. Start the hike on the left side of the building. Trailhead GPS: N34 29.633' / W85 37.045'; Falls GPS: N34 29.637' / W85 37.003'

The Hike

Lodge Falls can be accessed on a short trail that begins at the parking lot where you turn off Blalock Drive. It is a short but steep little climb down, which is why I have labeled it as being a moderate hike.

When you arrive and park, look for a gravel road on the far left side of the parking lot that wraps around one of the lodge buildings. Walk this road behind the building, crossing the headwaters of the falls over a footbridge. Then, as the trail winds its way in the opposite direction, cross the top of the falls itself over a second bridge.

A short trek steeply downhill from the DeSoto State Park lodge takes you to the dark walls of Lodge Falls.

After crossing, the trail becomes a dirt and rock path that makes a sharp right turn, heading steeply downhill until at mile 0.1 a side trail splits off to the right. Take this trail, and in only a few yards you will be at the base of the falls. When ready, turn around and retrace your steps to your vehicle.

28 Little River and Little Falls

One of the most spectacular and recognizable falls in the state is the 45-foot-tall block waterfall known as Little River Falls, and unless there is a severe drought, the river always puts on a roaring good show. A composite boardwalk at Little River Canyon Falls Park makes viewing the falls ADA accessible. From here a rocky, narrow footpath follows the canyon rim for great views of the canyon and the rapids of Little River, with a visit to Little Falls, a 10-foot-tall block waterfall with several different names that is a popular swimming hole in the summer.

Height of falls: Little River Falls, 45 feet; Little Falls, 10 feet
Type of falls: Block
Distance: 1.5 miles out and back
Difficulty: Easy
Hiking time: About 1 hour
Start: On the west side of Little River Canyon Falls Park at the kiosk
Trail surface: Short section of composite and cement boardwalk (ADA accessible), then sand and rock footpath
Best seasons: Year-round; open sunrise-sunset
Canine compatibility: Dogs permitted; leash required

Fees and permits: None
County: DeKalb
Land status: National preserve
Trail contact: Little River Canyon National Preserve, 4322 Little River Trail NE, Ste. 100, Fort Payne, AL 35967; (256) 845-9605; www.nps.gov/liri/
Maps: *DeLorme: Alabama Atlas & Gazetteer.* Page 27, A7; trail maps available on the NPS website
Special considerations: The swimming hole at Little Falls is great, but don't take a dip when the water level is high and the current swift. Heed all warning signs.

Finding the trailhead: From Fort Payne, at the intersection of US 11 and 5th Street NE, take 5th Street NE 0.4 mile and turn left onto AL 35 South. Travel 7.6 miles and turn right into the parking lot. The trailhead will be on your right, on the west side of the parking lot. There are picnic tables and room for 100 cars. Trailhead GPS: N34 23.710' / W85 37.559'; Falls GPS: Little River Falls, N34 23.708' / W85 37.603'; Little Falls, N34 23.323' / W85 37.212'

The Hike

Little River Canyon is one of the most popular tourist attractions in Alabama. The canyon has been scoured out from the top of Lookout Mountain over the millennia by its namesake river, forming the deepest canyon east of the Mississippi—600 feet deep in some areas—and it all begins right here at Little River Falls.

By the way, the unique thing about Little River, besides the waterfall and canyon, is that it is one of the few rivers in the country that actually flows almost entirely on top of a mountain.

Top: A rainbow decorates the spray from Little River Falls as it tumbles down the channel, continually forming the surrounding canyon, the deepest east of the Mississippi River.
Bottom: When Little River is high, Little Falls (aka Martha Falls or the Hippie Hole) looks more like a fast shoal than a waterfall.

The waterfall is a spectacular 45-foot-tall block-type falls. Early risers who visit the falls will be treated to a beautiful rainbow in the spray as the sun rises. It's hard to believe as you gaze at the waterfall that kayakers actually run it, but they do.

The hike begins as a cement walkway on the south side of the parking lot at a kiosk. Here the path splits off into two directions. For those with special needs or in

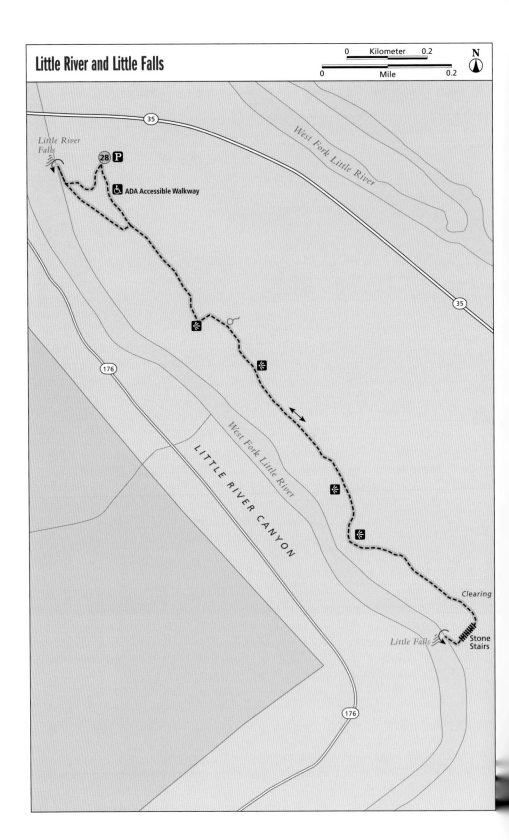

Little River and Little Falls

0   Kilometer   0.2

0   Mile   0.2

N

West Fork Little River

35

Little River Falls

28 P

ADA Accessible Walkway

176

West Fork Little River

LITTLE RIVER CANYON

Clearing

Little Falls

Stone Stairs

176

Little River Falls and Canyon are part of a 15,288-acre national preserve that protects the deepest canyon east of the Mississippi and one of the nation's Wild and Scenic Rivers, Little River. The river is one of the few that flows on top of a mountain. Besides hiking, kayaking, and a drive along the scenic highway around the rim, a trip to the canyon would not be complete without a visit to the Little River Canyon Center. The center was opened in 2009 and features historical exhibits, an HD theater showing documentaries, concerts, and frequent presentations on a wide variety of subjects. Learn more about the center by visiting the website at www.jsu.edu/epic/canyoncenter.

wheelchairs, the path to the left (south) is a ramp with handrails. The other path is straight ahead down a series of stairs. Either way, both paths lead to the canyon rim and the best view of the falls.

If you are disabled, return to the trailhead the way you came. For everyone else, head back the way you came, but instead of climbing the stairs, continue straight on the composite boardwalk and soon you will come to an opening where you begin your hike on the red-blazed dirt and rock footpath that follows the rim of the canyon downstream to Little Falls.

Little Falls is another one of those waterfalls with an identity crisis. Its official name is Little Falls. Some call it Martha's Falls (not sure of the story behind that one), while others know it as the Hippie Hole. The reason for that name is because behind the 10-foot block cascade there is a deep, cold, and very popular swimming hole.

The trail to Little Falls takes you past several overlooks with stunning views of the canyon and the rapids far below, but use caution on the bluffs. It's a long, rocky way down.

At mile 0.7 the trail comes out of the woods and into a clearing. This is the south end of the Little Falls Trail that comes in from the north. To get to the falls, you will need to cross the clearing to the southeast, make a right turn, and walk steeply down stone stairs to the falls and swimming hole. When ready, simply retrace your steps to the trailhead.

Miles and Directions

0.0 Start at the parking lot. The trail kiosk is located on the south side. The walkway forks at this point. The left fork is an ADA-accessible ramp. All others can take the right fork to the south down a set of stairs. At the bottom, turn right and arrive at the best view of Little River Falls. When ready, turn around and head southeast.

0.1 Continue walking straight southeast, passing the stairs you descended earlier.

0.2 Arrive at an opening in the walkway's handrail and begin walking the red-blazed dirt trail.

0.3 Come to an overlook on the right. In less than 0.1 mile, cross a small spring.

0.4 Come to a second overlook.

0.5 A short side trail to the right leads you to a third overlook.

0.6 Come to the fourth overlook.

0.7 Arrive at a clearing. Continue straight to the southeast. In less than 0.1 mile, turn right to begin walking steeply down a set of natural stone stairs.

0.8 Arrive at Little Falls. When ready, turn around and retrace your steps to the boardwalk.

1.4 Back at the boardwalk, walk through the opening you passed at mile 0.2 and turn right, taking the cement walkway to the trailhead.

1.5 Arrive back at the trailhead.

29 Graces High Falls

The deepest canyon east of the Mississippi—Little River Canyon—hosts the tallest waterfall in the state: Graces High Falls. This 133-foot plunge falls is spectacular to view from the overlook on AL 176, but remember, this is a very seasonal waterfall and can be no more than a trickle or even nonexistent when there is lack of rain. The overlook offers the chance for disabled and special-needs visitors to glimpse the beauty of the falls.

Height of falls: 133 feet
Type of falls: Plunge
Distance: Roadside
Difficulty: Easy
Hiking time: Less than 15 minutes
Start: Roadside overlook
Trail surface: Stone, gravel
Best seasons: Sept–May; open sunrise–sunset
Canine compatibility: Dogs permitted; leash required
Fees and permits: None

County: DeKalb
Land status: National preserve
Trail contact: Little River Canyon National Preserve, 4322 Little River Trail NE, Ste. 100, Fort Payne, AL 35967; (256) 845-9605; www .nps.gov/liri/
Maps: *DeLorme: Alabama Atlas & Gazetteer.* Page 21, G8; trail maps and canyon road maps available on the NPS website
Special considerations: The falls are very seasonal and rain dependent.

Finding the trailhead: From Fort Payne, at the intersection of US 11 and 5th Street NE, take 5th Street NE southeast 0.1 mile and turn right onto Godfrey Avenue NE. Travel 0.3 mile and turn left onto 1st Street. In 0.3 mile turn right onto Mountain Road SE. Travel 0.3 mile and merge onto Adamsburg Road/CR 78. Continue on CR 78 5.3 miles and turn right onto CR 255. In 0.2 mile, CR 255 becomes AL 176 West. Continue on AL 176 West 1.9 miles and the well-marked overlook will be on your left. There is room for about 15 cars. Trailhead/Falls GPS: N34 21.469' / W85 40.647'

The Hike

The overlook for Graces High Falls is right off the winding AL 176. The parking lot is gravel, while the walk at the railing and canyon rim is natural, flat (but uneven) stone.

There are a couple of trails down into the canyon where you could walk along the river to view the falls, but as they say when hiking canyons, what goes down must come up. This is the deepest canyon east of the Mississippi, and those trails are not for the faint of heart. Contact the National Park Service for information. One of those is the Eberhart Trail. The trailhead is located at Eberhart Point, only 0.5 mile south of the Graces High Falls overlook. The trail heads very steeply down into the canyon—a 354-foot drop over 0.4 mile—where it bottoms out on the banks of Little River. You can walk north up the creek about 400 feet and turn left (northwest) to follow Bear Creek about 0.5 mile to view the falls from below. Just remember, the hike back up is very difficult, even with benches along the route to take a break.

The turbulent ribbon cascade of Graces High Falls is believed to be the tallest such waterfall in the state.

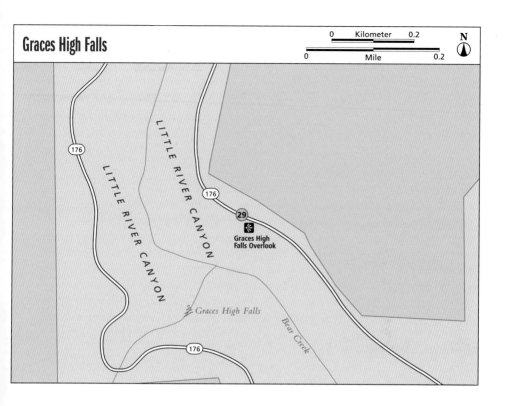

Graces High Falls

30 High Falls Park

An absolutely incredible waterfall can be found in a city park just south of Lake Guntersville in the town of Grove Oak—High Falls. This is one behemoth of a waterfall when Town Creek is really flowing. The falls are over 35 feet tall and up to 300 feet wide. To top it off, a section of the falls roars through a 25-foot-tall natural bridge.

Height of falls: 35 feet, 300 feet wide
Type of falls: Block
Distance: 0.8-mile lollipop loop
Difficulty: Easy
Hiking time: About 1 hour
Start: From the parking lot to the south
Trail surface: Paved, dirt, rock
Best seasons: Year-round; open 10 a.m.–6 p.m.
Canine compatibility: Dogs permitted; leash required
Fees and permits: None

County: DeKalb
Land status: City park
Trail contact: DeKalb County Tourism, 1503 Glenn Blvd. SE, Fort Payne, AL 35968; (256) 845-3957; https://visitlookoutmountain.com
Maps: *DeLorme: Alabama Atlas & Gazetteer.* Page 20, H3
Special considerations: After crossing the bridge over Town Creek, the hike to the bottom of the falls is a bit steep and narrow and may not be suitable for small children and dogs.

Finding the trailhead: From Grove Oak, at the intersection of CR 50 and CR 402, take CR 402 south 0.8 mile, where it becomes AL 227 South. Continue straight on AL 227 South 1.5 miles and turn right onto CR 356. Travel 0.8 mile and turn left onto CR 1905/CR 394. Travel 0.5 mile and turn right to stay on CR 394. Drive 0.7 mile and turn left onto CR 144. The parking lot will be ahead in 0.2 mile. Trailhead GPS: N34 24.078' / W86 03.979'; Falls GPS: N34 24.024' / W86 04.044'

The Hike

The hike to High Falls in the town of Grove Oak may not be as long and as difficult as some of our other treks, but it sure does deliver in the scenery.

Town Creek is what powers this block waterfall that stretches some 300 feet across when the creek is full. When it's really running, folks call it Alabama's own Niagara Falls.

You will have plenty of Kodak moments as you stroll the paved and gravel path along the rim of the gorge, including views of a beautiful natural arch that has been eroded away over centuries by the creek, the water flowing through the center of the natural bridge.

Your first breathtaking look at the falls comes a mere 0.1 mile into the hike. As mentioned, the trail is paved and an easy walker down to the rim of the gorge from the parking lot to that first view, but once you get there, the path is very close to the edge and the drop-off is dangerous to say the least, one that could result in an unhappy ending. Keep your kids close at hand and your dog on a leash.

Simply beautiful—the power of Town Creek in its full fury at High Falls Park. PHOTO COURTESY MALISA MAY

In 0.25 mile, you'll come to an interesting bridge that crosses the creek. This bridge was originally a covered bridge that was built in 1923 to facilitate trade with the growing city of Huntsville and Madison County. Sadly, the covered bridge was destroyed by fire in the 1950s, but through the efforts of city and county officials as well as many other organizations, the original piers of the bridge were put back into use in 1998, repurposed to make this walkway, which will give you some really nice views of the creek just above the falls.

If you would like to see the falls from its base, you can cross the bridge and turn right, heading rather steeply downhill on a rocky, narrow path that may be too much for small children and pets. Use caution.

Besides the spectacular falls, younger kids will enjoy the park's playground. And be sure to visit the park store where they have snacks, caps, and T-shirts for sale. The always friendly staff will be more than happy to tell you about the thrill seekers who come here to jump off the cliffs and plunge into the waterfall's pool. Full disclosure—I am not one of them.

One other note, the park closes promptly at 6 p.m. Thirty minutes before close, a siren sounds. Your vehicle could be towed and impounded if you're locked in, resulting in a hefty fine.

Miles and Directions

0.0 Begin from the parking lot to the south.

0.1 First view of the falls to your right. Use caution. The trail is very close to the edge.

0.2 A short gravel path leads you to the pedestrian bridge. Cross the bridge to the south. In less than 0.1 mile on the other side, turn right and carefully follow the narrow, rocky trail downhill.

The piers of a former 1923 covered bridge support the walkway across Town Creek at High Falls Park. PHOTO COURTESY MALISA MAY

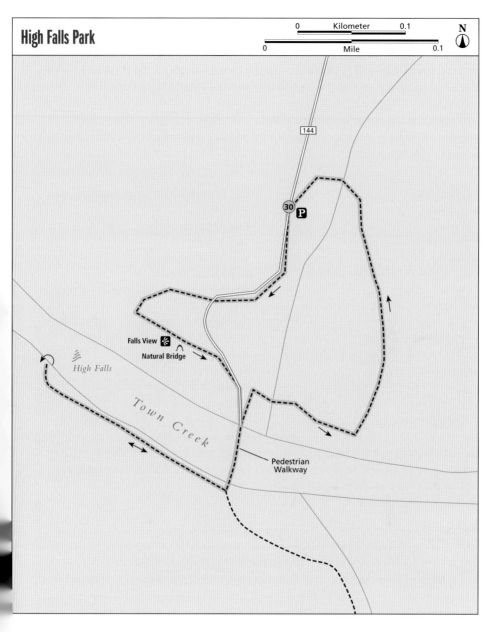

High Falls Park

Kilometer 0.1 / Mile 0.1 — N

144

30 P

Falls View

Natural Bridge

High Falls

Town Creek

Pedestrian
Walkway

0.4 Arrive at the base of the falls. When ready, turn around and retrace your steps across the bridge to the other side.

0.5 Once across the bridge, you can either turn to the right for a nice walk in the woods back to the trailhead or turn left to retrace your steps to the trailhead (the latter cuts the trip by 0.1 mile).

0.8 Arrive back at the trailhead.

31 Red Mill (Scarham Creek) Falls

With a long since abandoned red mill building in the background, Red Mill Falls is a very scenic and photogenic roadside waterfall at the confluence of Whippoorwill and Scarham Creeks in Albertville, Alabama. There are actually two waterfalls, one created where the old mill dam on Scarham Creek was located, the other a natural cascade on Whippoorwill.

Height of falls: 20 feet
Type of falls: Cascade
Distance: Roadside or short 100-foot hike
Difficulty: Easy
Hiking time: None
Start: View from the narrow parking area on Althea Nixon Drive
Trail surface: Pavement (roadside); dirt and rock to creek
Best seasons: Year-round (view may be obscured by foliage in spring and summer); open sunrise–sunset

Canine compatibility: Dogs permitted; leash required
Fees and permits: None
County: Marshall
Land status: Public
Trail contact: None
Maps: *DeLorme: Alabama Atlas & Gazetteer.* Page 26, B2
Special considerations: While this is a beautiful waterfall, leaves obscure the view from spring to early fall if you view it from the roadside. There is no trail here. If you do walk down the hillside to the creek, use extreme caution.

Finding the trailhead: From Guntersville, at the intersection of AL 227/Lusk Street and US 431, take AL 227 southeast 3.2 miles and turn right onto Hustleville Road. Travel 6.4 miles and turn left onto Martling Road. Travel 1.2 miles and turn right onto Althea Nixon Drive. A small dirt pull-off will be on the right. Park here. Trailhead GPS: N34 19.617' / W86 09.765'; Falls GPS: N34 19.607' / W86 09.718'

The Hike

Once an old mill, the old red building that stands at the junction of Whippoorwill and Scarham Creeks in Albertville seems like it has been there forever, or at least that's what locals will tell you. Today the building is slowly deteriorating, but still gives visitors to the falls a beautiful scene worthy of a postcard.

This is another one of those waterfalls with an identity crisis. Some call it the Scarham Creek Falls, while others call it Double Bridges since there are two bridges nearby. But it is more commonly referred to as Red Mill Falls.

If you want to view the falls from the roadside, the best time to visit is in late fall and winter when the leaves are down; otherwise the view is obscured.

You can take a 100-foot walk down to the banks of the creek from the parking pull-off, but there isn't a trail here. It's pick your own way, so use extreme caution due to some drop-offs.

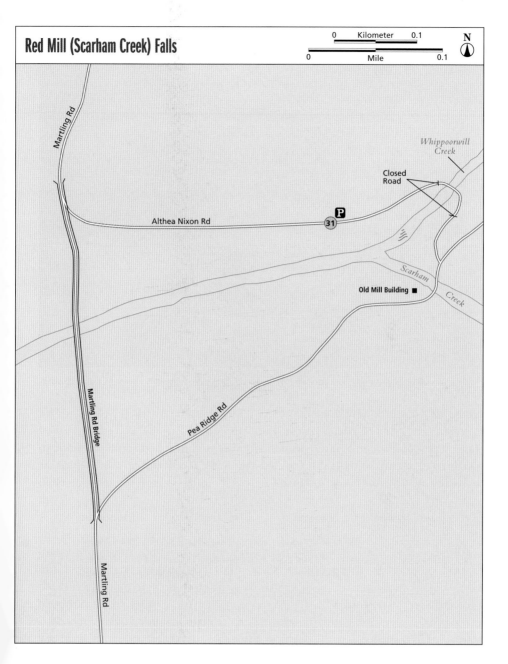

Althea Nixon Drive dead-ends just ahead of where you park, the bridge having been closed to traffic. You can walk across the bridge to view the top of the falls on Whippoorwill Creek, then take a look at the old building on the other side. I wouldn't recommend going inside, though. Its future is tenuous.

The view down Scarham Creek from the top of Red Mill Falls.

32 Shoal Creek Falls

Our second Shoal Creek, this one just northeast of Guntersville, is a picturesque roadside block-type waterfall. The falls are 50 feet wide and 15 to 20 feet tall. The best time to visit is when the creek is running full after plentiful rain and your view is not obscured by foliage. Even still, in late spring and early summer, the falls presents a true Kodak moment when it is framed with the greenery of the season.

Height of falls: 20 feet
Type of falls: Block
Distance: Less than 0.1 mile
Difficulty: Easy
Hiking time: About 15 minutes
Start: At the parking lot on the right side of Cooley's Grocery store (CG's)
Trail surface: Dirt
Best seasons: Sept–June; open sunrise-sunset
Canine compatibility: Dogs permitted; leash required

Fees and permits: None
County: Marshall
Land status: Public
Trail contact: None
Maps: DeLorme: Alabama Atlas & Gazetteer. Page 25, A9
Special considerations: Since you're using CG's parking lot to view the falls, be courteous and stop in to buy a Coke or something.

Finding the trailhead: From Guntersville, at the intersection of US 431 and AL 69, take AL 69 south 6.1 miles and turn right onto Union Grove Road. Travel 2.3 miles and turn right onto Snow Point Road. CG's Grocery Store will be on the left. Park on the far right side of the building. Trailhead GPS: N34 23.387' / W86 25.452'; Falls GPS: N34 23.387' / W86 25.452'

The Hike

Shoal Creek Falls (also known as Neighbor's Mill Falls) is a great little—OK, not little—block-type waterfall. The best time to view it is when the river is running full from fall through spring, but it is a beautiful sight even in summer.

The waterfall can be viewed by parking on the extreme right side of Cooley's Grocery Store (better known as CG's) on Snow Point Road. The view from here is stunning in fall and winter but a bit obscured at other times of the year due to the thick foliage. However, there are a couple of short trails that you can walk to get a better view any time of the year from the top of a bluff.

The first trail is a short 100-foot path straight ahead to the north from where you park that takes you to a small clearing. Use caution on the bluff.

The second is a short road walk up Snow Point Road. From your car, turn right and walk carefully up the narrow shoulder of the road to the north. In about 150 feet, there is a small, nondescript trail on the left (overgrown and hard to discern when brush is growing) that leads to another clearing (if you pass the only mailbox on the right, you missed it).

Spring greenery frames the view of Shoal Creek Falls.

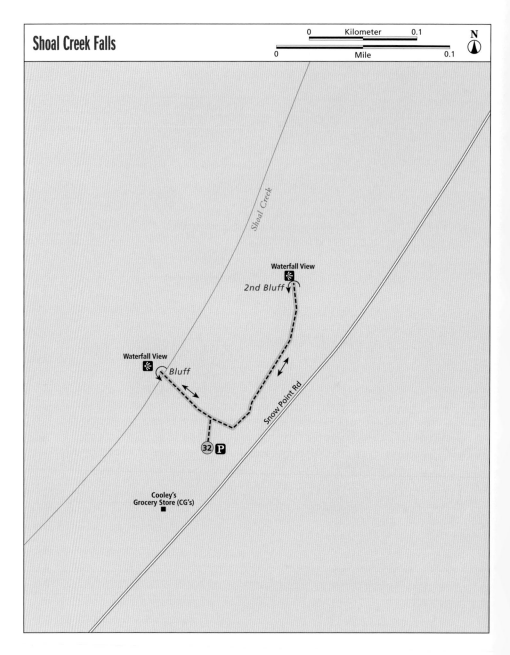

Turn left onto the trail here and travel a few yards to a second bluff and view. Again, use caution. When ready, retrace your steps back to the trailhead.

33 Hurricane Creek Park

Five trails lead you into an amazing gorge cut by the rushing waters of Hurricane Creek and to several unnamed waterfalls that cascade down its rocky face in this park just north of Cullman in Falkville. The seasonal waterfalls cascade over tall sandstone bluffs, with a few tumbling over rock shelters where you can walk behind the curtains of water. At the base of the gorge is a wonderful swimming hole formed by a long-abandoned dam. And there are many other surprises in store on this hike, including a natural bridge and Twilight Tunnel, a totally dark walk through a cave, perfect for the explorer in you.

Height of falls: Several falls of varying heights, tallest 40 feet
Type of falls: Plunge
Distance: 2.2-mile double loop with extension
Difficulty: Difficult
Hiking time: About 2 hours
Start: From the patio at the old park entrance building to the southeast of the parking lot
Trail surface: Packed dirt studded with rocks and roots
Best seasons: Sept–June; open sunrise–sunset
Canine compatibility: Dogs permitted; leash required
Fees and permits: None

County: Morgan
Land status: City preserve
Trail contact: Hurricane Creek Park, 22550 2nd Ave. NW, Falkville, AL; (256) 735-9157; https://cullmanrecreation.org/facilities-parks/hurricane-creek-park/
Maps: *DeLorme: Alabama Atlas & Gazetteer:* Page 24, A4; park map available on the park's website
Special considerations: Average hikers shouldn't have a problem hiking down and back up from the gorge, but keep in mind that it is a steep descent and ascent. The falls are very rain dependent.

Finding the trailhead: From the intersection of I-65 at exit 308 and US 278/4th Street SW in Cullman, head east on US 278/4th Street SW for 1.4 miles. Stay to the left at the fork onto Main Avenue SW. Travel 0.6 mile and turn left onto US 31 North/2nd Avenue NW. Travel 7.9 miles and the parking lot will be on the right. You will see a building to the southeast. Head to the building and walk around the right side, crossing the patio. This is the trailhead. Trailhead GPS: N34 17.206' / W86 53.698'; Falls GPS: Main falls, N34 17.315' / W86 53.537'; others scattered throughout the hike

The Hike

This hike uses five separate trails—Hurricane, High, Creek, South Ridge, and North Highland—to complete a double loop featuring several nice seasonal falls, a natural bridge, tall bluffs, and a cooling swimming hole. At the time of this writing, the trails were not blazed and have very little signage. They intertwine, making it difficult at times to figure out which trail you're on and a bit frustrating if you're trying to stay on a specific route. Just relax, explore, and enjoy the ramble.

The hike in and out of the gorge is a steep and rocky climb. You may want to use the option described in Miles and Directions if you have children or dogs with you. The option is still steep, but it cuts the hike down to 1 mile and you will have an easier go of it while still visiting the main waterfall, the picnic area, and the swimming hole.

The hike begins at the old park entrance building. Walk around the right side of the building, crossing a patio, and on the other side, arrive at the intersection of the North Highland and Hurricane Trails. We'll begin this hike by taking a right onto the Hurricane Trail, which is rated difficult by Cullman City Parks and Recreation—and they aren't kidding. If you opt to take the optional route described in the Miles and Directions, go straight instead of turning.

As you head downhill there is an interesting artifact on your right—an abandoned cable car that was once used to haul visitors to the bottom of the gorge and swimming in Hurricane Creek. The trail down has a thick canopy and is lined with wildflowers in season.

Your first waterfall comes at mile 0.2. You will find yourself walking beneath a rock shelter behind the water curtain of the two-tier falls (remember, the falls are seasonal and rain dependent). Soon you will cross the rushing waters of Hurricane

Walk behind the curtain of this waterfall in a U-shaped rock shelter at Hurricane Creek Park.

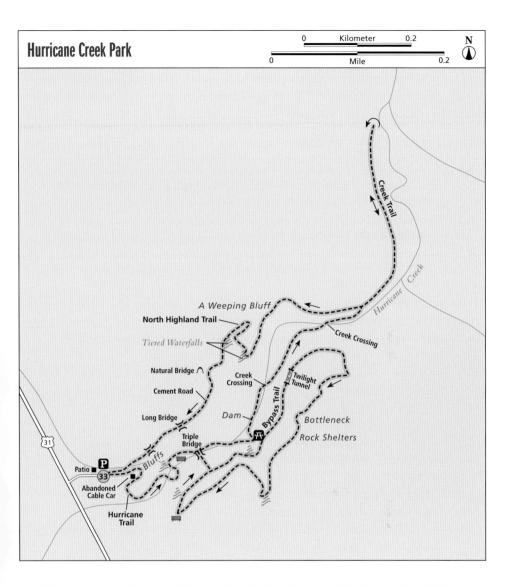

Creek at mile 0.3 over a triple wooden bridge that resembles long pallets. After crossing, turn to the right, and in less than 0.1 mile, you will cross the base of a second waterfall over a 20-foot bridge. Keep heading to the northeast.

Three more waterfalls are found on the route—another walk-behind plunge at mile 0.7, a multi-tiered cascade shortly after that, and finally the main tiered cascade, a 40-foot tumble down a craggy rock face at mile 1.9. Here the trail uses a series of wooden platforms and stairs to make sharp switchbacks up the waterfall to the top.

An interesting geologic feature is encountered just 0.4 mile into the hike—Twilight Tunnel. If you're claustrophobic or afraid of the dark, this isn't for you. You can use the Bypass Trail around the tunnel to the left to avoid it; otherwise, step into the cave and pause a moment to let your eyes adjust before continuing. The trail comes out on the other side.

One other attraction that draws people to Hurricane Creek Park is the picnic area at mile 1.1, with picnic tables and the low, cascading waterfall formed by an old dam that makes a deep, cold swimming hole.

Miles and Directions

0.0 Start by walking around the right side of the old park entrance building, crossing the patio, to arrive at the intersection of the North Highland Trail (straight ahead) and Hurricane Trail (to the right). Turn right (east) onto the Hurricane Trail

0.2 Walk under a rock shelter behind a two-tier waterfall. In less than 0.1 mile, turn right (southeast) at the "To Twilight Tunnel/South Ridge Trail" sign.

0.3 Cross the creek over a triple wooden bridge. On the other side turn right (southwest) onto the Ridge Trail. In less than 0.1 mile, pass another waterfall on the right, crossing its runoff over a short 20-foot bridge.

0.4 Arrive at the Twilight Tunnel.

0.6 Arrive at the Bottleneck.

0.7 Walk beneath a rock shelter and waterfall as the trail follows the U shape of the bluff canyon.

0.9 Pass another multi-tiered waterfall. A set of switchbacks takes you down a set of stairs made of railroad ties.

1.0 Cross the creek and turn right (northeast).

1.1 Arrive at the picnic area and swimming hole. Turn right onto the Creek Trail.

1.5 This is the turnaround for the Creek Trail.

1.8 Turn right to the north west: look for a sign that reads, "High Trail Long Way Back to Park." Continue north.

1.9 The trail uses a series of sharp switchbacks to take you uphill at the main tiered waterfall.

2.0 Arrive at a sandstone natural bridge on the right.

2.1 Come to the upper end of a cement road. Turn right onto the road, following it only about 100 feet to where the trail leaves the road to the left (southwest). In less than 0.1 mile, cross a narrow, 60-foot-long bridge over a drop-off.

2.2 Cross a 150-foot bridge over a fast-moving stream. In less than 0.1 mile, arrive back at the trailhead.

Option: For an easier walk, instead of starting on the Hurricane Trail, go straight from the patio at the entrance building on the North Highland Trail. Reverse the miles and directions above from mile 2.2 to the picnic area, making this a nice 1-mile out-and-back hike where you can visit the main waterfall and the swimming hole. When ready, turn around and retrace your steps to the trailhead.

34 Mardis Mill Falls

Pull off the road and take this short walk down a hillside to a beautiful wide cascade, Mardis Mill Falls. This block cascade churns down its rocky base to fill a deep cool pool, a favorite swimming hole complete with rope swing to send you sailing into the basin (check that the rope is safe before attempting).

Height of falls: 15 feet tall, 35 feet wide
Type of falls: Block
Distance: 0.1 mile out and back
Difficulty: Easy
Hiking time: Less than 5 minutes
Start: On the south side of the parking lot on the gravel and rock path
Trail surface: Gravel, flat rock
Best seasons: Year-round; open sunrise–sunset
Canine compatibility: Dogs permitted; leash required

Fees and permits: None
County: Blount
Land status: Public
Trail contact: Friends of the Locust Fork River, PO Box 638, Cleveland, AL 35049; (205) 274-3537; www.friendsofthelocustforkriver.org
Maps: *DeLorme: Alabama Atlas & Gazetteer.* Page 25, F8
Special considerations: The Friends of the Locust Fork do an excellent job of keeping the trail clean, but there still can be some trash. Bring a bag along to help keep it clean.

Finding the trailhead: From Blountsville, at the intersection of CR 26 and US 231/Main Street, take US 231/Main Street south 3 miles. Turn left onto Mardis Mill Road. Travel 0.7 mile and the gravel parking area will be on the right. There is room for 6, maybe 7, cars comfortably. If there are more, just be sure not to block the road. The trail begins on the south side of the parking area. Trailhead GPS: N34 02.711' / W86 34.284'; Falls GPS: N34 02.670' / W86 34.272'

The Hike

Mardis Mill Falls is the perfect example of a block-type waterfall with its low height and 35-foot-wide footprint, its water cresting over the top of the rock wall to fill a deep, inviting pool below that's been a favorite swimming hole for locals for who knows how long. It can get crowded in the summertime, so plan to arrive early.

The falls are hidden away just down a hillside off a backroad in Blount County along Graves Creek. You may hear some people also refer to it as Graves Creek Falls. The parking lot is a long and narrow gravel pull-off on the side of Mardis Mill Road. There is a trash can here to help keep this access point clean, provided courtesy of the Friends of the Locust Fork River (FLFR). The group does an excellent job of maintaining and protecting access to not only this branch but also many of the tributaries and the main flow of the Locust Fork River, one of the longest free-flowing rivers remaining in the country. The volunteers work hard to make sure the waterways are clean and safe for all recreational users. If you can, please visit their website (see Trail contact) and become a member, make a donation, or volunteer to lend a hand.

The Friends of the Locust Fork River have made it easy to visit this beautiful roadside cascade—Mardis Mill Falls.

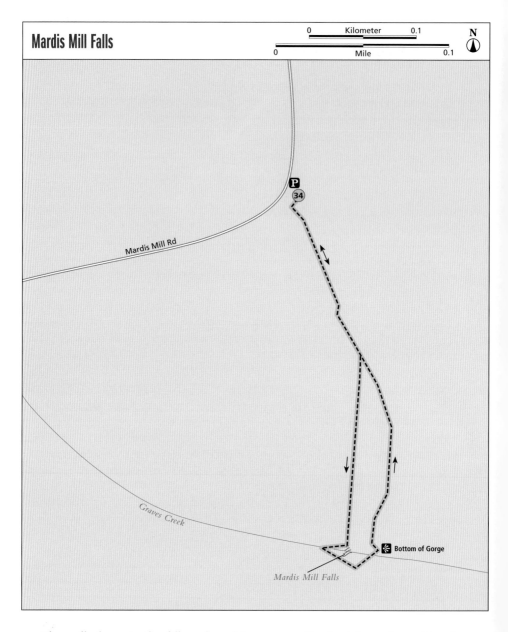

Mardis Mill Falls

P
34

Mardis Mill Rd

Graves Creek

Bottom of Gorge

Mardis Mill Falls

The walk down to the falls and pool is very easy. Begin right at the parking lot and follow the large, flat rocks downhill to the south. If its damp out, the rocks can be a little slippery so be careful. In less than 0.1 mile, you're at the falls. When you're ready to leave, just turn around and head back the way you came.

35 Noccalula Falls

An incredible hike to, and under, a beautiful plunge waterfall—the 90-foot Noccalula Falls in Gadsden. This hike takes you along a paved path high above the historic gorge for incredible views of the waterfall from above, before heading down to the bottom on a rock and dirt path that leads you right to the base of the falls for an up-close and personal view and a walk behind the curtain of water in one of the deepest rock shelters you will find.

Height of falls: 90 feet
Type of falls: Plunge
Distance: 1.6 miles out and back (first 0.2 mile ADA accessible)
Difficulty: Easy to moderate with slippery rocks at falls and a moderate climb out of the gorge
Hiking time: About 1.5 hours
Start: At the south side of the northern parking lot
Trail surface: First half paved, then rock and dirt footpath in gorge
Best seasons: Year-round, better fall–late spring
Canine compatibility: Dogs permitted; leash required

Fees and permits: None
County: Etowah
Land status: City park
Trail contact: Noccalula Falls Park and Campground, 1500 Noccalula Rd., Gadsden, AL 35904; (256) 549-4663; www.noccalulafallspark.com
Maps: *DeLorme: Alabama Atlas & Gazetteer.* Page 26, F3; additional trail maps available on the park's website
Special considerations: It's fun to walk beneath the falls but very slippery. Don't walk behind the falls when it's at full flow.

Finding the trailhead: From the intersection of I-65 exit 183 and US 431/US 278 in Gadsden, take US 431/US 278 east 2.5 miles and turn left onto Kyle Avenue. Travel 0.5 mile and make a sharp left turn onto 12th Avenue. In 0.1 mile take the left fork onto Noccalula Road/Woodcliff Road. Travel 1.3 miles and turn left onto Mann Drive and the parking lot. The trail begins in the southwest corner of the parking lot. Trailhead GPS: N34 02.524' / W86 01.267'; Falls GPS: N34 02.461' / W86 01.304'

The Hike

Noccalula Falls was named for Cherokee Indian princess Noccalula. Her story is as old as mankind itself, a love story with a tragic ending much like *Romeo and Juliet, Anna Karenina,* or *Wuthering Heights.*

As the story goes, a tribe of Cherokee Indians lived near what was then called Black Creek Falls. The tribe's leader was a powerful chief in early northeast Alabama. His daughter was said to have been the most beautiful in the land and was famed for her "loveliness of character."

Most of the time, you can walk behind the curtain of Noccalula Falls. This is not one of those times. Photo courtesy Eric Wright

Many men vied for the hand of the young princess, but she was in love with only one man, a warrior from their own tribe. Her father had other plans and arranged for Noccalula to marry a young warrior from a powerful neighboring tribe.

Noccalula's lover was banished from the tribe, and before long, it was wedding day. According to the story Noccalula awoke that morning to the birdsong she loved so much. Attendants helped her dress in wedding attire and then escorted her to the wedding feast.

Sometime during the feast, the princess, who was grieving for her lost love, slipped away unnoticed into the woods. Some say the soothing, rushing sounds of Black Creek Falls drew her to the water. She stood at the edge for a moment, then with one leap jumped over the edge to the gorge floor below.

When word arrived of his daughter's death, Noccalula's father went into grieving and at that moment renamed the falls "Noccalula Falls."

The waterfall is an incredible plunge waterfall. When the creek is full and swift it produces a thunderous sound that echoes down the gorge. The rock shelter it rushes over is deep and provides an amazing view from behind the curtain of water.

The route described here is a relatively easy jaunt for most members of the family, including those who have disabilities or special needs. They will not be able to walk the trail at the bottom of the canyon, but the first 0.2 mile, where they will have a spectacular view from the rim of the gorge, is paved.

A couple of reminders: First, when you arrive at the bottom of the falls, the rocks can be extremely slippery as you walk behind the curtain of water, so use caution.

Also, Black Creek can channel a lot of water down its course. Do not attempt to go behind the falls when the creek is flooding. And while it is a pretty easy walk, some may find the hike out of the gorge a little difficult. Take your time, enjoy the bluffs and creek, and you should be fine.

The un-blazed trail starts at the southwest corner of the parking lot, which is located only a few yards away from the top of the falls. Simply follow the paved and cement walkway south, crossing Black Creek and the upper falls a few hundred feet from the start. After crossing Black Creek, the footpath swings southwest to begin in earnest following the rim of the gorge.

There is an optional route to the falls, a 2.5-mile out-and-back that uses the Black Creek Trail, which follows the north side of the gorge and creek. It is a much more natural trail. You can learn more about this route by visiting the Noccalula Falls Park website or by contacting the park office (see Trail contact).

Miles and Directions

0.0 Start at the southwest corner of the parking lot and follow the paved and cement walkway south, crossing Black Creek and the upper falls in a few hundred feet. In less than 0.1 mile, pass the Princess Noccalula statue.

0.2 Pass the old gorge entrance and stairway on the right.

0.4 Turn right and follow a cement ramp to the bottom of the gorge.

A couple takes in the view behind Noccalula Falls during a time of very low flow.

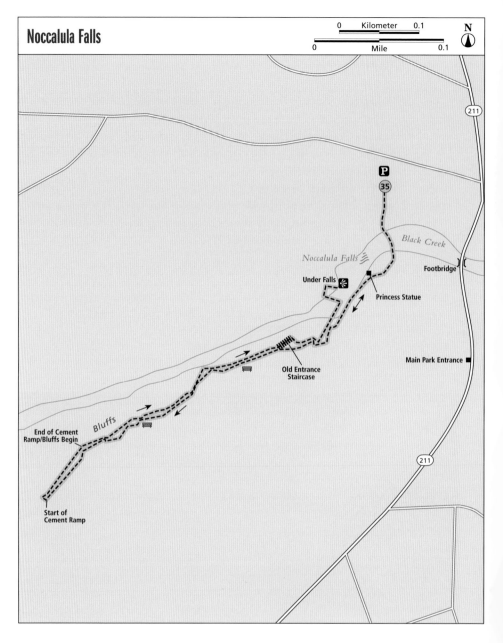

0   Kilometer   0.1

0   Mile   0.1

N

Noccalula Falls

Black Creek

Footbridge

Under Falls

Princess Statue

Old Entrance
Staircase

Main Park Entrance

Bluffs

End of Cement
Ramp/Bluffs Begin

Start of
Cement Ramp

0.5   The ramp ends and the trail becomes a rock and dirt footpath with tall bluffs on the right and Black Creek on the left. Pass a bench in less than 0.1 mile.

0.6   Pass a bench on the right.

0.7   Pass the bottom of the old entrance stairway on the right.

0.8   Arrive at the falls. When ready, turn around and retrace your steps to the trailhead.

1.6   Arrive back at the trailhead.

North Alabama Honorable Mentions

F. Greg's Two Falls

A rain-dependent waterfall in Little River Canyon is this hidden little two-tier gem—Greg's Two Falls. The waterfall is simply beautiful when water is plentiful, especially in the spring and summer when the azaleas and mountain laurel are in full, colorful bloom framing its frothy flow.

The walk down to the falls is only 0.3 mile, but there isn't a real trail here, only a faint path down from the highway along the banks of Wolf Creek, which forms the falls. It is a steep walk with some drop-offs so use extreme caution. Park your vehicle near the bridge on AL 176. There are only very narrow grass shoulders here, so use caution parking your vehicle so that you don't get stuck while still parking far enough off the roadway. From here, follow the creek down 0.1 mile to the upper falls and an additional 0.2 mile to view the lower falls. Trailhead GPS: N34 22.224' / W85 39.755'; Falls GPS: N34 22.054' / W85 39.759'

G. Point Rock Falls

Buck's Pocket State Park in Guntersville has seen a recent rebirth as an ORV (off-road vehicle) park, but there are still a few great hiking trails available like this difficult, boulder-strewn, 2.3-mile out-and-back hike that leads to a seasonal waterfall at Point Rock. This waterfall is rain dependent. If the water is very low, the falls disappear underground to continue feeding Little Sauty Creek far below.

Begin at the park office and head west on the park road. In 0.2 mile, turn left onto the trail and begin the climb. In 0.5 mile, arrive at what is known as the Big Sink, with the falls on your right. A short side trail in 0.1 mile leads directly to the falls. But don't stop here. Keep walking up the slope for a breathtaking view of the gorge from the top of Point Rock at an overlook. Trailhead GPS: N34 28.563' / W86 02.752'; Falls GPS: N34 28.369' / W86 02.858'

H. Poison Ivy Falls

Here's another chance to visit the roiling waters of the West Fork of Little River at DeSoto State Park and a little-known cascade called Poison Ivy Falls. It's probably not on many people's radar because it is a very, and I mean very, seasonal waterfall, but after a good rain, it is beautiful.

The falls are accessible via the Gilliam Loop Trail, which is located about 2 miles south of the Lodge Falls (hike 27) trailhead at the end of Cabin Road. This 2.4-mile out-and-back hike begins to the east of the trailhead. Soon you will arrive at the first trail junction with the DeSoto Scout Trail (DST). This is called "Exit 1." Turn left onto the DST. This portion of the hike starts out easy enough, then heads steeply downhill from a ridge until it reaches the river. At the river, turn right (south) and follow the DST about 0.5 mile to arrive at the base of the falls. When ready, turn around and retrace your steps to the trailhead. Trailhead GPS: N34 29.400' / W85 36.775'; Falls GPS: N34 29.183' / W85 35.905'

I. Rattlesnake Saloon

You've never seen a waterfall like this before. It's not only the beautiful naturally occurring waterfall that drives visitors here, but also the restaurant that is located underneath its curtain of water! You heard right. In 2009, under a tall, deep rock ledge, the Foster family constructed a restaurant and bar. After a good rain, a 60-foot plunge waterfall flows over the ledge, giving you a unique dining experience. The property also has several hiking and equestrian trails that lead to other waterfalls as well. Visit their website for details at www.rattlesnakesaloon.net/s. Trailhead/Falls GPS: N34 38.893' / W87 54.449'

J. Stephens Gap

What is described as one of the Southeast's most beloved caves offers up an unbelievable hike—the Southeastern Cave Conservancy's Stephens Gap Callahan Cave Preserve. Once again, this hike requires a "surface permit" available through SCCI. The permit is free and restricts you to only hiking the trail, no rappelling or serious caving allowed (visit the SCCI website for information at www.saveyourcaves.org).

Much like hike 17 (Lost Sink) and hike 21 (Neversink Pit), the Gap is another example of karst geology. Stephens Gap is a 143-foot-deep pit that cavers love to rappel down. For hikers, a steep 0.7-mile hike (1.4 miles out and back) up the mountain leads to a walk-in passageway that will take you to a view of the interior of the cavern and the falls from 50 feet above the cave's floor. The hike is very slippery and the drop-off precarious, so use extreme caution. Good boots are a must, and a headlamp and helmet are recommended. Trailhead GPS: N34 40.125' / W86 13.383'; Falls GPS: N34 40.612' / W86 13.699'

K. Welti Falls

Just southeast of Cullman is an incredible waterfall that is formed by Brindley Creek as it flows from Forest Ingram Lake. It's a 100-foot-wide, 20-foot-tall cascade called Welti Falls. This is an easy to moderate 1-mile out-and-back hike that will take you right to the base of the waterfall, but be sure to visit when the lake is full and topped out so that you are guaranteed an amazing water show when you arrive. Sadly, the ease of access from the highway means that many people visit the falls and leave their trash behind. Please be a good neighbor and bring along a trash bag to help keep the area clean.

To find the trailhead, begin at the intersection of US 278 and 3rd Street in Cullman. Travel 0.2 mile and turn right onto 3rd Avenue. Drive 0.8 mile and turn left onto 11th Street SE. Drive 0.8 mile, making a slight right onto CR 703/Welti Road. Continue 4 miles. Just after you cross the bridge over Eight Mile Creek, there is a pull-off on the left (north) side of the road. Park here. From here you may (or may not) see a faint, nondescript trail heading downhill. Follow it down; otherwise, carefully pick your way down. When you reach the creek, there is an old, rutted road that heads to your right (northeast). Follow it along the creek bed. If you can't find it, simply follow the creek upstream. In only 0.5 mile, you will arrive at the falls. Use caution; the rocks are slippery. When ready, turn around and retrace your steps to the trailhead. If you come to the bridge at the confluence of Brindley and Eight Mile Creek, you've gone about 300 feet past the turn to head uphill to your car. Trailhead GPS: N34 08.708' / W86 46.017'; Falls GPS: N34 08.962' / W86 45.826'

L. Yellow Creek Falls

And now for something completely different—a kayak trip to Yellow Creek Falls, a spectacular 100-foot cascade with pool. Bring your own kayak or rent one from the Yellow Creek Falls Fish Camp (visit them online at https://yellowcreekfalls.com for information). From the fish camp, paddle northwest up the wide creek 0.1 mile and pass the remains of an old stone railroad trestle. Continue upstream another 0.2 mile and securely tie your boat off. From here, an obvious footpath heads up through the rocky gorge about 0.25 mile to the base of the falls. Trailhead GPS: N34 13.336' / W85 43.443'; Falls GPS: N34 13.543' / W85 43.726'

Central Alabama

Heading farther south, we arrive at Alabama's central region, which stretches from just north of Montgomery to just north of Birmingham. The waterfalls in this region are not as numerous as they are in the north region, but they are impressive nonetheless. In fact, many hikers consider them some of the most scenic in the state. You be the judge.

Geologically speaking, this region is part of what is known as the Piedmont Plateau, an area that is known to have the oldest rocks and soils in the western hemisphere, being formed by volcanoes millions of years before the Appalachian Mountains were pushed up into existence.

Speaking of the Appalachians, everyone knows that Alabama has mountains stretching as far south as the town of Wetumpka, which is only 20 miles north of Montgomery, but many do not realize that these mountains make up the southern terminus of the Appalachian Mountain range that runs up the east coast of the United States all the way to Canada. Many of the waterfalls we will explore in this region are tucked away within the friendly boundaries of the Talladega National Forest and its designated wilderness areas.

Within the forest's boundaries you will find some incredible waterfalls that are Appalachian worthy, and they are all centered around the state's highest mountain, Cheaha.

Topping out at 2,407 feet, Cheaha Mountain and its famous state park make a great base camp to explore these waterfalls from. Within only a few minutes' drive of the park, you will find yourself deep in the forest, leaving civilization and the winding mountain roads behind to explore beautiful, shimmering lakes, a rushing mountain stream with dozens of cascades, and two impressive waterfalls including the tiered cascade Cheaha Falls (hike 44) and the amazing Devils Den (hike 43) with its turbulent rocky flow into Lake Chinnabee, which offers plenty of swimming opportunities and a breathtaking view of the long, churning cascade from high above along a wooden walkway clinging to a rock face.

We will also climb ladders and stairs up the side of a rock bluff to view the three tiers of High Falls (hike 41) and hike a portion of Alabama's famous long path, the Pinhoti Trail, for a truly secluded 50-foot cascade along Little Hillabee Creek (hike 37). And that's only a preview!

The churning waters of Cheaha Creek heading toward Devils Den.

Heading even farther south we'll venture to one of the most popular state parks in Alabama, Oak Mountain, to visit its centerpiece, Peavine Falls (hike 47), which thunders down a narrow gorge when it's full. And there are many more, lesser known, waterfalls in the area to explore, including the 90-foot plunge of Falling Rock Falls (hike 48) and the many cascades that line the trails of Moss Rock Preserve (hike 46).

The weather in the central region provides pleasant hiking fall through spring. In the fall you will be treated to the brilliant color changes over the landscape, hike in light blankets of snow in winter, and in spring, hike along mountain ridges dotted with blooming and fragrant dogwood, mountain laurel, and native azalea.

As you would expect, the hottest temperatures arrive around July when daytime highs average 91°F and 71°F at night. And then there is that humidity, but it just doesn't seem as bad when you're on a mountain. Or is that just a frame of mind thing? Heat indexes can still skyrocket into triple digits, so pack plenty of water.

In winter, you can expect snow and ice here as temperatures average from 55°F in the day to 33°F at night, but temps in the single digits are not uncommon.

If you'd like to camp while you're exploring the waterfalls, you can rough it with backcountry camping in Talladega National Forest, where you can camp almost anywhere as long as you follow forest service guidelines (see Appendix A: Camping in the National Forests of Alabama).

If you'd rather not rough it, your two best options are at Oak Mountain State Park where there are plenty of improved tent campsites (with water and power), RV sites, and primitive campsites, and Cheaha State Park where the campsites and cabins have been recently renovated. Cheaha also boasts a thirty-room hotel and a cliffside swimming pool with one of the most incredible views around located right next to their restaurant.

Learn more about lodging in Alabama State Parks by visiting www.alapark.com.

36 Turkey Creek Falls

This is not a towering waterfall but a beautiful, short cascade that flows swiftly over the smoothed boulders and shelves of the 25-foot-wide Turkey Creek. Turkey Creek Falls is one of the most popular swimming holes in the state and can be very crowded in the summer as people take a refreshing dip in one of its pools or tube over one of the waterfall's chutes.

Height of falls: 6-foot main drop
Type of falls: Cascade Block
Distance: 0.1 mile out and back
Difficulty: Easy
Hiking time: About 10 minutes
Start: At the south side of the Turkey Creek Nature Preserve's parking lot
Trail surface: Rocky footpath
Best seasons: Year-round; open 9 a.m.–5:30 p.m. Wed–Sun; 7 a.m.–9 a.m. Fri–Sat; closed Mon and Tues; pedestrians only (by foot or bike)
Canine compatibility: Dogs permitted; leash required

Fees and permits: None
County: Jefferson
Land status: Alabama Forever Wild tract
Trail contact: Turkey Creek Nature Preserve, 3906 Turkey Creek Rd., Pinson, AL 35126; (205) 680-4116; www.turkeycreeknp.com
Maps: *DeLorme Alabama Atlas & Gazetteer.* Page 31, B7; trail maps available on the park's website
Special considerations: When swimming, use caution on the slippery rocks. The flow can be pretty fast and there are deep pools behind some of the rocks that could be dangerous for small children.

Finding the trailhead: From Birmingham on I-59 exit 128 take AL 79 north 10.4 miles. Turn left onto CR 131/Narrows Road. In 0.2 mile, turn right onto Turkey Creek Road (a one-way loop road) and follow it 0.7 mile. The trailhead will be on the left. Trailhead GPS: N33 42.171' / W86 41.781'; Falls GPS: N33 42.127' / W86 41.821'

The Hike

Operated and maintained by the city of Pinson and protected by the Alabama Forever Wild program, this 462-acre tract was preserved specifically to ensure the survival of several rare and endangered species of darter fish that call the creek's cool, clear, and fast-flowing waters home. But while saving these rare fish, the town and state have also opened the tract to the public so they can experience this incredible water show.

In the spring and summer, the swimming hole beneath the falls can get pretty crowded, so plan on arriving early or take in the preserve during the cooler months to avoid the crowds. If you plan on taking a swim, you will find changing rooms and restrooms for your convenience at the parking lot. There are actually two pools along the creek that you can swim in, one just off the road and another a little farther north on the creek. Just follow the bank to get there.

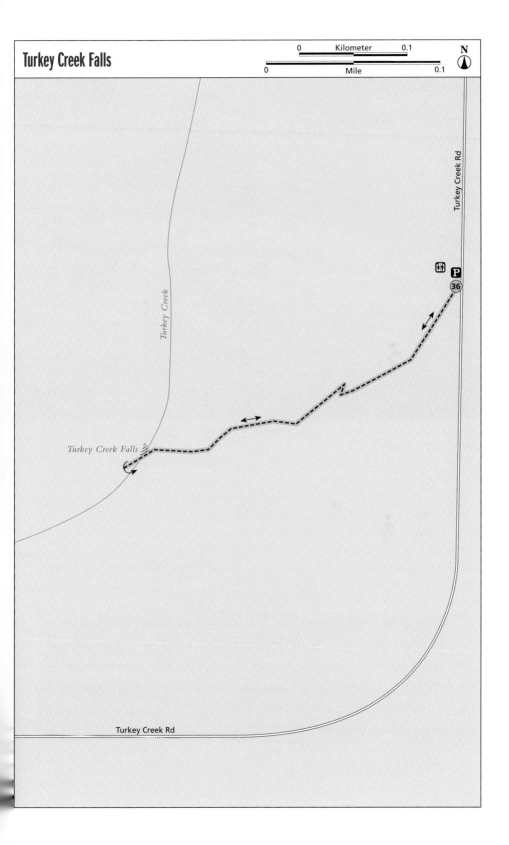

Turkey Creek Falls

Turkey Creek Rd

Turkey Creek

Turkey Creek Falls

Turkey Creek Rd

The cool, clear, and swift-flowing waters of Turkey Creek are the home of the endangered vermillion darter.

And while you're here, bring along the bike or hiking boots and take a trek along one of the preserve's 5-plus miles of trail that wind their way over ridges above the creek and past huge rock outcroppings along the creek itself.

The trail to the falls is a short 0.1-mile out-and-back walk from the parking lot on Narrows Road. Cross the road to the southwest. On the other side, a short set of stairs leads you down to Turkey Creek, the falls, and great swimming. When ready, retrace your steps to the parking lot.

Because of Alabama's unique patchwork of geologic and hydrological features, the state has the most diverse aquatic life in the country. Alabama has more species of fish, snails, mussels, crayfish, and turtles than any other state. Three rare and endangered species of fish live in the waters of Turkey Creek—the watercress, rush, and the vermillion darter. One of these, the vermillion, can only be found here in Turkey Creek, right in the middle of the most populous county in the state, Jefferson.

37 Little Hillabee Falls

If you're looking for solitude, a walk in the woods where you will have the trail practically to yourself, and a hike that culminates in a spectacular mesmerizing cascade, then lace up your boots and take this trek to Little Hillabee Falls, a sparkling 50-foot-tall cascade found deep in the Talladega National Forest on Alabama's famous long path, the Pinhoti Trail.

Height of falls: 50 feet
Type of falls: Cascade
Distance: 3.2 miles out and back
Difficulty: Easy
Hiking time: About 1.5 hours
Start: At the pull-off at FS 515
Trail surface: Short gravel road, dirt and rock footpath
Best seasons: Sept–June; open sunrise–sunset
Canine compatibility: Dogs permitted; leash required
Fees and permits: None

County: Cleburne
Land status: National forest
Trail contact: Talladega National Forest, Talladega Ranger District, 1001 North St., Hwy. 21 N., Talladega, AL 35160; (256) 362-2909; www.fs.usda.gov/detail/alabama/about-forest/districts/?cid=fsbdev3_002555; Pinhoti Trail Alliance, www.pinhotitrailalliance.org
Maps: *DeLorme: Alabama Atlas & Gazetteer.* Page 33, D7
Special considerations: Just enjoy. It's a great hike through the hardwoods.

Finding the trailhead: From Cheaha State Park, take AL 281 north 12 miles. There will be a gravel pull-off on the left at FS 515. Park here but don't block the gate to the service road. There is plenty of room for 10 cars. The trail begins behind the gate to the west using FS 515. Trailhead GPS: N33 34.521' / W85 41.454'; Falls GPS: N33 34.188' / W85 42.420'

The Hike

This hike begins by using the dirt and gravel FS 515 as an approach trail for 0.5 mile. Even though this section is on a dirt road, the walk isn't bad, with a good canopy overhead providing shade in the warmer months.

In only 0.5 mile you will turn left off the road and begin hiking Alabama's famous long path, the Pinhoti Trail (PT). The Pinhoti stretches over 171 miles from Flagg Mountain in Weogufka, Alabama, to the Georgia state line where it meets up with the Georgia Pinhoti Trail and eventually connects to the Appalachian Trail.

The Pinhoti (which is a Native American word for "turkey home") is blazed with dollar bill–size blue paint markings and sporadically with white metallic diamond markers tacked to trees with the image of a turkey foot and "NRT" (National Recreational Trail) emblazoned on them. You really won't need the blazes. The narrow footpath is well worn and well maintained by local volunteers with various organizations, including the Pinhoti Trail Alliance (see Trail contact).

Little Hillabee Falls

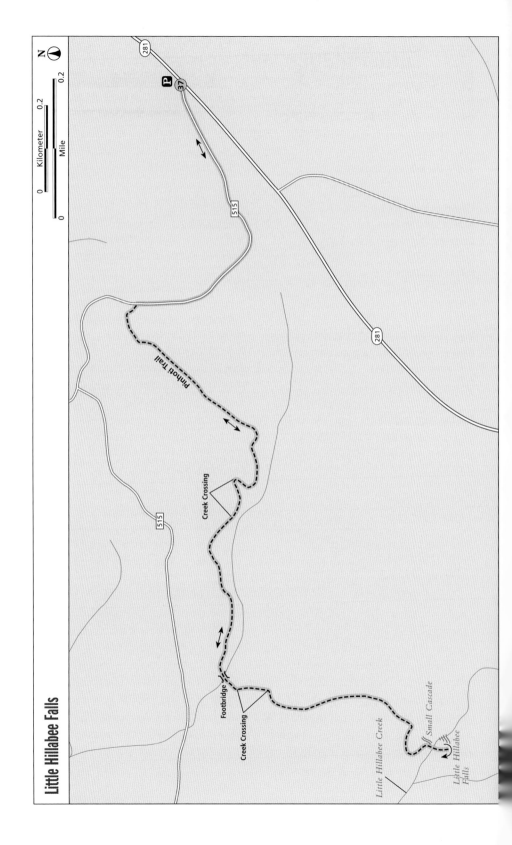

A trek down Alabama's famous long trail, the Pinhoti, is rewarded with a visit to the tall cascade known as Little Hillabee. PHOTO COURTESY MICHAEL MARTIN

The hike described here is along a part of section 7 of the long path. If you're looking for something a bit longer, there are two additional options you can try that are outlined in the Miles and Directions.

The hike itself is over gently rolling hills all the way to the falls, with the exception of one moderate but very short climb at mile 1.2. There is an interesting creek crossing at this point, where the creek flows underground for a couple of yards at the point where you cross it before popping out on the opposite side.

The trail winds around a hollow until mile 1.6, where you will first hear the cascading waters then round a bend and arrive at your destination.

Miles and Directions

0.0 Start at the metal gate that blocks FS 515, heading around the gate to the right.

0.5 Turn left (west) onto the Pinhoti Trail.

0.9 Cross a creek and in less than 0.1 mile, cross another.

1.1 Cross a 12-foot wooden footbridge over a creek.

1.2 Cross another creek, then in a few yards cross another that disappears underground.

1.5 Cross a creek with a nice little cascade.

1.6 Arrive at the falls. When ready, turn around and retrace your steps to the trailhead.

3.2 Arrive back at the trailhead.

Option: To make this into a 5.4-mile out-and-back hike with a little more challenging terrain, continue driving up AL 281 an additional 0.5 mile and turn right onto CR 131. Travel 0.6 mile and turn left onto US 431 North. Travel 0.7 mile. A pull-off for parking will be on your left. Pick up the PT here and head south on the trail. For a good 17.6-mile point-to-point overnight, start at the southern end of section 7 at the Cheaha Trailhead and end at the trailhead just described on US 431 North. Visit the Pinhoti Trail Alliance website for details (see Trail contact).

38 Angel Falls

A nice cascade waterfall with incredible views of the surrounding Talladega Mountains awaits you atop the tallest mountain in the state, Cheaha, on this 1-mile out-and-back hike. Angel Falls is very rain dependent, so make sure to visit after a good soaking rain. Along the way you will also see the handiwork of the Civilian Conservation Corps (CCC) from the 1930s in the hand-carved stone steps and reservoir.

Height of falls: 40 feet
Type of falls: Cascade
Distance: 1.0 mile out and back
Difficulty: Moderate
Hiking time: About 1 hour
Start: From the north side of the cul-de-sac where you park; trailhead is across the road.
Trail surface: Dirt and rock footpath, short gravel road
Best seasons: Sept–Apr; open sunrise-sunset
Canine compatibility: Dogs permitted; leash required

Fees and permits: Day-use fees
County: Clay
Land status: State park
Trail contact: Cheaha State Park, 19644 AL 281, Delta, AL 36258; (256) 488-5111; www .alapark.com/parks/cheaha-state-park
Maps: *DeLorme: Alabama Atlas & Gazetteer.* Page 32, E5; trail maps available at the camp store or on the park's website
Special considerations: The Rock Garden has a precipitous drop; use caution.

Finding the trailhead: From Lineville at the intersection of East Main Street and AL 49, take AL 49 north 14.2 miles. Turn left onto AL 281 South. Travel 3.4 miles and turn right onto Bunker Loop. Pay your entrance fee either at the camp store located right at this turn or at the gate a few yards north. Bunker Loop is a one-way road that loops around the top of the mountain. Follow it around for 1.8 miles and make a sharp left turn onto the Chalet Road. The cul-de-sac and parking will be straight ahead in 0.2 mile. Park on the narrow grass strip off the road. The trailhead is to the north across the road. Trailhead GPS: N33 29.059' / W85 48.767'; Falls GPS: N33 28.870' / W85 48.855'

The Hike

The path described here is a moderate walk over a rocky footpath that leads to breathtaking views of the mountains from what is appropriately called the Rock Garden, a jumble of boulders and a towering rock bluff, and to the uppermost section of the waterfall. The hike uses two trails. We will begin on the pink paint–blazed Mountain Laurel Trail. The path begins directly across the street to the north from where you park in the cul-de-sac. The park uses the "dit-dot" method of blazing, which means that at sharp turns, two blazes—one on top of the other—are painted on a tree. The top blaze is offset showing the direction in which the trail turns.

The second trail is the blue-blazed Lake Trail. Signs call it the Lake Trail, while some of you old-timers will remember it as being called the Rock Garden Trail. This

Angel Falls spills down the rock face of the Rock Garden. PHOTO COURTESY MANDY PEARSON

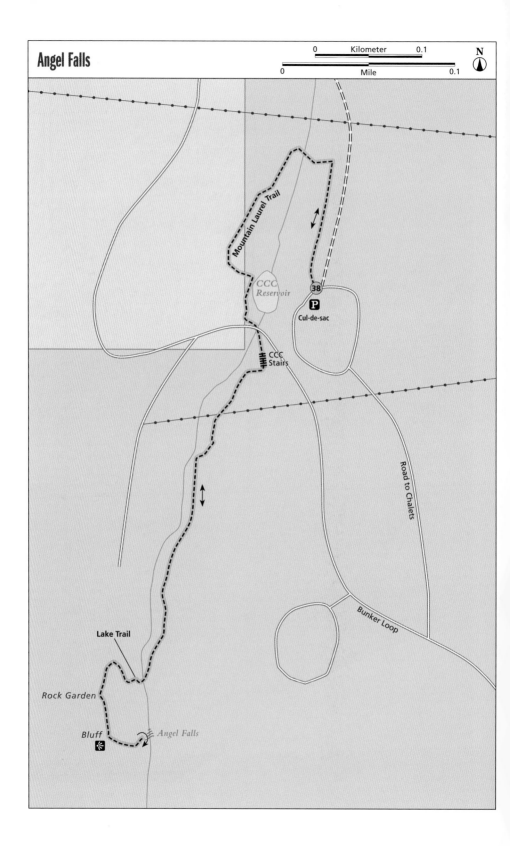

Angel Falls

0   Kilometer   0.1

0   Mile   0.1

N

Mountain Laurel Trail

CCC
Reservoir

38

P

Cul-de-sac

CCC
Stairs

Road to Chalets

Bunker Loop

Lake Trail

Rock Garden

Bluff

Angel Falls

A thick cloud descends over the state's tallest mountain, Cheaha, on the way to Angel Falls.

path is extremely rocky and steep and is rated difficult if you go all the way to the bottom of the falls. The views from the bluffs are spectacular. In fact, you can see the opposite trailhead about a mile away at the bottom of the mountain. But these bluffs are dangerous. This hike is not recommended for small children, and be sure to keep older children and dogs away from the edge. There is an easier way to view the top of the falls, which I'll mention in the Miles and Directions.

At just about the halfway mark of the hike, you will turn left off the Lake Trail and follow the base of a tall bluff where you will have breathtaking views of the Talladega Mountains and arrive at the top section of the falls. For this description, we turn around here and head back to the trailhead, but you can access the bottom of the falls by continuing on down the Lake Trail a short distance. Just remember, you have to come back up.

Along the way, you will pass the CCC reservoir built in the 1930s. The reservoir was made by cutting and laying each stone by hand. When the reservoir is full, a nice little waterfall spills out, making a very picturesque scene.

Miles and Directions

0.0 Start across the street from the cul-de-sac on the Mountain Laurel Trail. In less than 0.1 mile, turn left, leaving the gravel road.

0.1 Come to a Y and take the left fork.

0.2 Arrive at the CCC reservoir. Follow along the right side of the stone wall and head toward the road (Bunker Loop). Carefully cross the road, picking up the trail again on the other side to the south. In less than 0.1-mile, walk down stone CCC-built steps where you will come to the creek. Do not cross it. Turn left to stay on the trail.

0.3 Cross under powerlines.

0.4 Come to an intersection with a sign that shows Angel Falls is to the left (see option below). Take the right fork and cross the creek. On the other side, turn right. In a few yards, turn left onto the blue-blazed Lake Trail. In less than 0.1 mile, leave the Lake Trail and turn left (west), following the base of a large rock bluff.

0.5 Arrive at the top of Angel Falls. Carefully scamper to the stream for a good view. When ready, turn around and retrace your steps to the trailhead.

1.0 Arrive back at the trailhead.

Option: You can take an easier walk to view the top section of the falls by taking the left fork at mile 0.4 and walking an additional 400 feet. You can then turn around and head back to the trailhead from there.

39 Shinbone Falls

This is not the prettiest of hikes with the first mile of the trek being on a dirt and gravel road, but what it lacks in scenery along the approach trail is more than made up for as you bushwhack down a hillside to the incredible horsetail cascade known as Shinbone Falls. One of the best times to visit is late spring through early summer when pink and white mountain laurel frame the falls.

Height of falls: 30 feet
Type of falls: Horsetail cascade
Distance: 2.4 miles out and back
Difficulty: Easy
Hiking time: About 1 hour
Start: From the northwest side of the narrow parking area at the gate
Trail surface: Gravel and dirt road
Best seasons: Sept–June; open sunrise–sunset
Canine compatibility: Dogs permitted; leash required
Fees and permits: None
County: Clay

Land status: National forest
Trail contact: Talladega National Forest, Talladega Ranger District, 1001 North St., Hwy. 21 N., Talladega, AL 35160; (256) 362-2909; www.fs.usda.gov/detail/alabama/about-forest/districts/?cid=fsbdev3_002555
Maps: *DeLorme: Alabama Atlas & Gazetteer:* Page 33, F6
Special considerations: The first mile is a dirt and gravel road with no canopy that can be brutal walking in the heat of summer. Use caution heading down to the falls. There is no real trail.

Finding the trailhead: From Cheaha State Park, head north on AL 281 for 3.4 miles. Turn right onto AL 49 South and travel 3.1 miles. The narrow pull-off for parking will be on the right. There is enough room for 5 cars comfortably. Trailhead GPS: N33 27.137' / W85 46.599'; Falls GPS: N33 27.652' / W85 47.413'

The Hike

Named for its location, Shinbone Valley, Shinbone Falls is a little-known gem of a horsetail cascade in the Talladega National Forest that is well worth the trek even if the approach trail to the falls is a little, let's say, void of features.

I will be the first to admit it. When I parked the car and started heading to the falls, I was underwhelmed. The first mile of this hike is on a dirt and gravel road that weaves its way through an area that was clear-cut for its pines. The good news is that there are young, 5-foot-tall saplings returning along the roadside that brighten up the hike with their lush green needles. The bad news—there is no canopy, so if you hike this trail in the summer, the sun can be brutal. But don't let that initial walk keep you from visiting. The falls are more than worth it.

Begin this hike at the pull-off on AL 49 by walking around the metal gate to the northwest. The only tricky part of this hike comes at mile 1.0, where the road widens into an open dirt "cul-de-sac" and appears to end, but it doesn't. Continue on to the

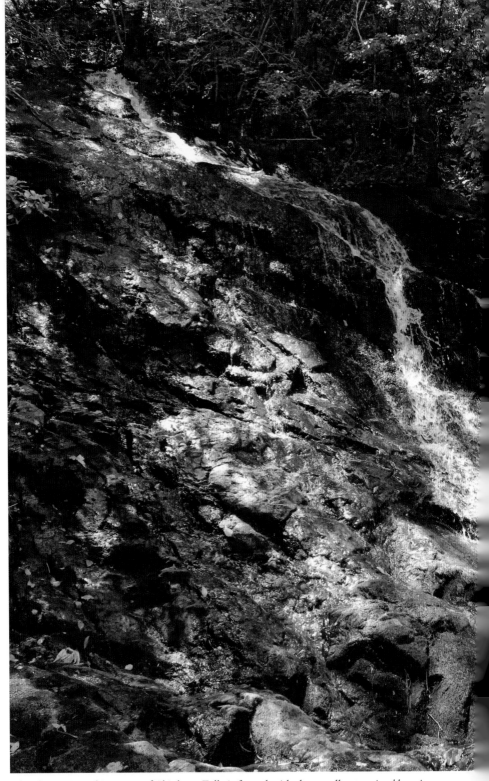

The glimmering white water of Shinbone Falls is framed with the equally stunning blooming mountain laurel.

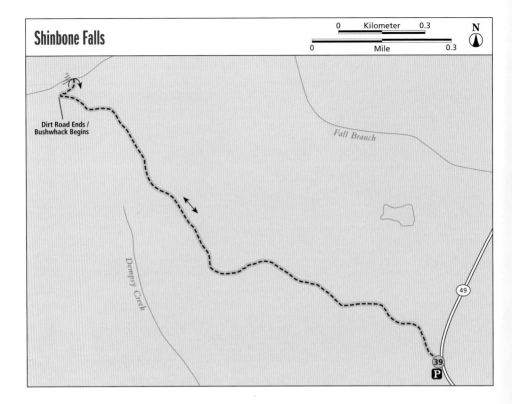

west/northwest and you will see the overgrown remnants of the road. Keep following it for another 0.1 mile to where it really does dead-end. Here you should see a boulder to your right. This is where the bushwhacking begins and you carefully make your way downhill to the falls.

The waterfall cascades down its rocky bed into a very narrow gorge. In the spring and summer, the falls are framed in blooming and fragrant white and pink mountain laurel, quite the reward for your effort.

Miles and Directions

0.0 Start at the pull-off on AL 49 and head northwest, walking around the metal gate.

0.6 Pass a dirt road coming in from the left.

0.7 Good view of surrounding mountains.

1.0 Come to where the road widens. The dirt road continues to the west/northwest and is overgrown.

1.1 The road ends. There is a boulder to your right. Bushwhack past the boulder to the northeast. You should find a small footpath that leads to the falls; otherwise, very carefully, head cross-country downhill to the falls.

1.2 Arrive at the falls. When ready, retrace your steps to the trailhead.

2.4 Arrive back at the trailhead.

40 Nubbin Creek

Situated in the Talladega National Forest and Cheaha Wilderness, there is an incredible underrated trail that features three amazing waterfalls, the Nubbin Creek Trail. Within 1.5 miles or so of the trailhead, you will encounter a breathtaking long cascade that churns into a turquoise pool and two additional cascades that rumble down their boulder-strewn channels.

Height of falls: Gorge Falls, 100 feet; other cascades, 40 feet
Type of falls: Cascade
Distance: 3.2 miles out and back
Difficulty: Moderate
Hiking time: About 2 hours
Start: At the east side of the Nubbin Creek trailhead parking lot
Trail surface: Dirt, rock
Best seasons: Sept–June; open sunrise–sunset
Canine compatibility: Dogs permitted; leash required
Fees and permits: None

County: Clay
Land status: National forest wilderness area
Trail contact: Talladega National Forest, Talladega Ranger District, 1001 North St., Hwy. 21 N., Talladega, AL 35160; (256) 362-2909; www.fs.usda.gov/detail/alabama/about-forest/districts/?cid=fsbdev3_002555
Maps: *DeLorme: Alabama Atlas & Gazetteer:* Page 32, F6
Special considerations: The side trail to the gorge is moderately steep, but the drop-off at the bluff is precipitous. Use caution and keep children away from the edge.

Finding the trailhead: From Lineville at the intersection of AL 9 and AL 49, take AL 49 north 10.7 mile and turn left onto Nubbin Creek Road (there is a brown USFS sign pointing the way at the turn). In 0.8 mile the pavement ends. Continue another 2.3 miles. The parking area will be on the right and is well marked. Trailhead GPS: N33 24.940' / W85 48.356'; Falls GPS: Gorge Falls, N33 25.202' / W85 48.489'; Waterfall 1, N33 25.445' / W85 48.932'; Waterfall 2, N33 25.667' / W85 48.950'

The Hike

The Nubbin Creek Trail is a steady, moderate climb up the side of Talladega Mountain. It isn't too difficult, but some will find hiking around the rocky waterfalls to get a better view and the climb up from the gorge view a bit strenuous but not unmanageable.

The Nubbin Creek Trail itself is actually a 4-mile point-to-point path that connects to other trails in the wilderness, making it the perfect access for a backpacking adventure, but when it comes to waterfalls, the first 1.5 miles are the best and that's the hike we will take here.

All three waterfalls are best experienced from September to June, with fall foliage igniting the landscape in fall and wildflowers gracing the path in spring. You can see the falls in the dog days of summer, especially after a good rain, but otherwise they are only a shell of their former selves during those hot, dry months.

When full, the second waterfall along the Nubbin Creek Trail thunders down its boulder-strewn channel.

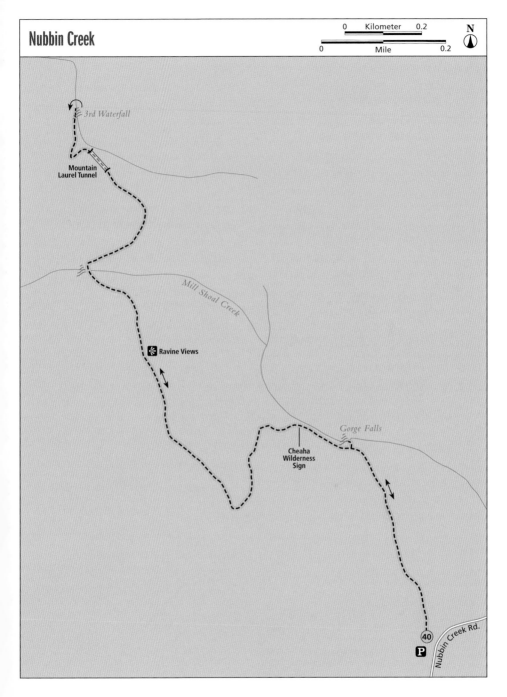

The trail is a narrow dirt and rock-strewn path with longleaf pines, white oaks, and thick brush giving the path an enclosed feeling. When you hike the trail in the spring, you will find yourself walking through a few "tunnels" of beautiful white mountain laurel.

From the parking lot it is difficult to see where the trail actually begins. It is inset a few yards into the woods on the east side of the parking lot. You know you're on the right path if you see a hiker sign a few feet in. From there the trail is un-blazed, as is the practice in wilderness areas, but it is well worn and very easy to follow.

At mile 0.3, you will pass a small side trail on the right and hear the first cascade in the gorge. Don't take this path. Continue straight to the northwest another five yards or so and come to the actual trail to the overlook. It is a steep, mountain laurel–lined path downhill to the bluff. The long, 100-foot (maybe more) cascade here is stunning as it churns through the gorge, ending in a turquoise pool. Use caution around the edge. It's a long way down.

You will have a couple of small creek crossings, nothing insurmountable, along the remainder of the route until at mile 1.2 you will arrive at the second falls—a churning tumble down a boulder-filled channel. The bank on the opposite side is a muddy 4-foot climb to get to the other side. You may want to do a little jog off-trail down the creek bed, where you'll have an easier time of it.

Our last waterfall and the turnaround for this hike comes at mile 1.6, another rocky cascade that is the perfect spot to just sit and reflect.

Miles and Directions

0.0 Start on the right (east) side of the parking lot. In a few yards come to a mileage sign.

0.3 You will hear the falls in the gorge to the right as you pass a short side trail on the right. Don't use this trail. Continue down the trail another few yards and come to a second trail. Take this short unmarked path downhill to a bluff to view the gorge and falls far below. When ready, turn around and return to the main trail. Turn right and continue to the northwest.

0.5 Mill Shoal Creek flows swiftly on your right (north.) Pass the Cheaha Wilderness sign.

1.2 Come to the second waterfall. Cross the stream to the northeast. The bank on the opposite side is a 4-foot muddy climb. Pick your way.

1.3 Nice views of the ravine to the right (southeast) in the winter.

1.5 Walk through a tunnel of mountain laurel.

1.6 Come to the third waterfall. When ready, turn around and head back to the trailhead.

3.2 Arrive back at the trailhead.

41 High Falls

A short but oh so memorable hike goes to High Falls in the Talladega National Forest, a three-segment cascade that can be a challenge to get to after heavy or sustained rainfall. The lower tier is a long cascade that tumbles down its boulder-strewn bed. The trail crosses this flow at its base, and when the stream is at full speed and flowing swiftly, it is a challenging crossing. Both the middle and upper tiers are beautiful 10- to 15-foot cascades, with the upper tier plummeting into a pool.

Height of falls: 45 feet over 3 tiers
Type of falls: Cascade and plunge
Distance: 0.6 mile out and back
Difficulty: Moderate
Hiking time: About 1 hour
Start: On the northeast side of the High Falls trailhead parking lot
Trail surface: Rock, gravel with a climb up a ladder
Best seasons: Sept–June; open sunrise–sunset
Canine compatibility: Dogs permitted; leash required
Fees and permits: None

County: Clay
Land status: National forest
Trail contact: Talladega National Forest, Talladega Ranger District, 1001 North St., Hwy. 21 N., Talladega, AL 35160; (256) 362-2909; www.fs.usda.gov/detail/alabama/about-forest/districts/?cid=fsbdev3_002555
Maps: *DeLorme: Alabama Atlas and Gazetteer.* Page 32, F5
Special considerations: Use caution crossing the flow on the lower tier when the creek is high.

Finding the trailhead: From Lineville at the intersection of CR 9/East Main Street and AL 49, take CR 9 west 300 feet and turn right onto 2nd Avenue North. In 200 feet, turn left onto Talladega Street. Travel 0.8 mile and turn right onto Highland Road. Travel 5.8 miles (along the way, Highland becomes Watershed Road then Highland again) and turn left onto Clairmont Springs Road. Drive 0.7 mile and turn right onto FS 650/High Falls Drive. The parking and trailhead will be ahead in 0.3 mile. Trailhead GPS: N33 22.220' / W85 50.585'; Falls GPS: Lower, N33 22.320' / W85 50.489'; Upper, N33 22.344' / W85 50.453'

The Hike

A fun but steep and rocky hike in the Talladega National Forest leads to one of the forest's most popular waterfalls, High Falls. The waterfall itself has three tiers, with the first being a long slide cascade down a rocky channel. The other two are nice plunge falls into collecting pools.

The trail we will use—High Falls Trail—basically parallels the branch that creates the waterfall as it heads steadily uphill from the trailhead. Although it's a short hike (only 0.6 mile total), High Falls can provide a few challenges when hiking to the uppermost tier.

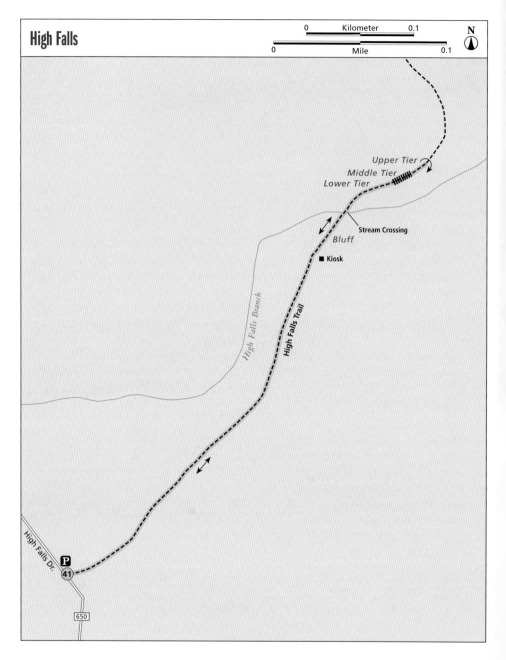

It begins easy enough on a wide gravel path following the base of a towering rock bluff with large chunks of its face littering the side of the trail. Only 0.2 mile into the journey, you will arrive at the base of the lower tier. Carefully pick your way across the stream to reach the other side. If the water is high, this can be a challenge and dangerous. Use your best judgment.

Sometimes crossing the flow of the lower tier of High Falls is challenging.

On the other side, the climb begins in earnest up the rocky trail that leads to the middle tier and then up a set of wood and steel stairs to the upper tier. The base of the upper tier is the turnaround for this hike, but you can continue a little bit farther and view the upper tier from the top of the falls by following a second set of stairs up the rock face. (**Note:** At that point, the High Falls Trail ends and the Odum Scout Trail begins.)

Miles and Directions

0.0   Start on the northeast side of the trailhead. The trail is a wide gravel road. In a few yards it will Y. Take either fork—the left fork follows High Falls Branch; the right follows the base of a tall bluff.

0.2   Pass the trail kiosk and arrive at the lower tier of the falls. Carefully cross the stream and, on the other side, turn right to head steeply uphill next to the branch. In less than 0.1 mile, arrive at the middle tier, then climb the wood and steel stairs to reach the upper tier.

0.3   At the top of the stairs, arrive at the upper tier. When ready, turn around and retrace your steps to the trailhead.

0.6   Arrive back at the trailhead.

Option: When you reach the upper falls, you can climb a second set of stairs to view the upper level from the top of the falls.

42 Hopeful Falls

A short and easy, level walking hike takes you to a little-known waterfall hidden away in the Talladega National Forest—Hopeful Falls. This 35-foot plunge falls doesn't disappoint, even in times of low water flow when a double ribbon courses down its rocky wall. When the water is really flowing, a solid curtain drapes across the rock shelf.

Height of falls: 35 feet
Type of falls: Plunge
Distance: 0.6 mile out and back
Difficulty: Easy
Hiking time: About 30 minutes
Start: Across the street from the parking area to the east of the 7-ton bridge
Trail surface: Dirt footpath with 4 stream crossings
Best seasons: Sept–June; open sunrise-sunset
Canine compatibility: Dogs permitted; leash required

Fees and permits: None
County: Talladega
Land status: National forest
Trail contact: Talladega National Forest, Talladega Ranger District, 1001 North St., Hwy. 21 N., Talladega, AL 35160; (256) 362-2909; www.fs.usda.gov/detail/alabama/about-forest/districts/?cid=fsbdev3_002555
Maps: *DeLorme: Alabama Atlas & Gazetteer:* Page 32, E4
Special considerations: Be careful on the thick, slick moss at the base of the falls.

Finding the trailhead: From Cheaha State Park, take AL 281 south 1.5 miles and turn right onto Cheaha Road. Travel 9.1 miles and turn left onto Bass Lane. Follow Bass Lane for 0.5 mile and come to the 7-ton bridge. Don't cross the bridge. Instead, park in the narrow pull-off to the right just before the bridge. There is room for 3, maybe 4, cars to park here. The trail can easily be seen across the road to the east. Trailhead GPS: N33 28.895' / W85 54.553'; Falls GPS: N33 28.971' / W85 54.357'

The Hike

This is a short and easy trek for hikers of all stripes to a little-known (except to locals, that is) waterfall—Hopeful Falls.

This is another one of those waterfalls with an identity crisis. On Google Maps it's called Hidden Falls. Some hikers call it the Camp Mac falls because of its proximity to the summer camp of the same name. Still others call it Secret Falls. But its more common name is Hopeful Falls, so named for the little community it is located in, Hopeful, Alabama.

Park your vehicle just before the 7-ton bridge on Bass Lane, but be sure to pull far enough off the road so you don't block traffic. The easily discernable, un-blazed trail begins directly across the street to the east. The path starts as a 2-foot-wide dirt path, but after the first creek crossing it widens considerably. The entire hike is a flat walk to the waterfall.

Even during times of low water, Hopeful Falls puts on a dazzling show.

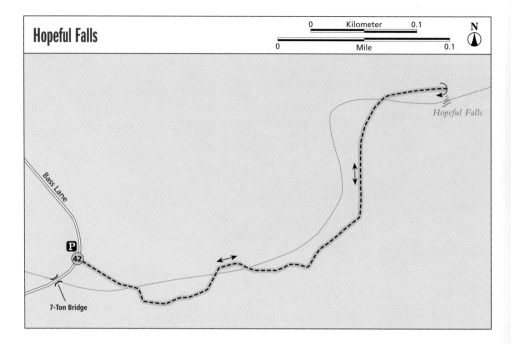

You will have to cross a creek four times on this hike. The first comes only 200 feet into the journey where there is a large 5-foot-wide tree that had fallen across the 10-foot-wide creek. A set of stairs were built to help you climb up on it. If you're uncomfortable with crossing via the tree, the creek is usually not very deep and the water clear, so you can keep your footing and wade across.

The trail winds its way back and forth across the creek until it finally arrives at the 35-foot-tall plunge falls. In times of low water, a double ribbon tumbles down the rock wall, losing touch with it only a few feet from the bottom. When the rains are plentiful, a curtain of water rumbles down. The pool at the bottom is not so much a swimming pool as it is a wading pool. Still, it's a great place to kick off the boots and cool your feet beneath this spectacular hidden waterfall.

Miles and Directions

0.0 Start at the trailhead across the street to the east from where you parked. In 200 feet, cross the creek over the felled tree or ford the shallow stream.

0.1 Rock-hop the creek.

0.2 Cross the creek again. In less than 0.1 mile, cross it again.

0.3 Arrive at Hopeful Falls. When ready, retrace your steps to the trailhead.

0.6 Arrive back at the trailhead.

43 Devils Den and Lake Chinnabee Spillway

Everything that makes the Talladega National Forest so beautiful is on full display along the Chinnabee Silent Trail and this hike to Devils Den—the shimmering waters of Cheaha Creek as it rushes toward Lake Chinnabee with its many shoals, cascades, and drops; the refreshing pools below those drops inviting you to take a dip in the cool mountain stream; and an incredible view of Devils Den Gorge from high above on an elevated bluff walkway. As a bonus, the Lakeshore Loop trail takes you to an impressive Civilian Conservation Corps (CCC)–built spillway on the far side of the lake.

Height of falls: Devils Den, average 15 to 20 feet; dam, 20 feet

Type of falls: Devils Den, tiered cascade; spillway, tiered dam

Distance: 3.3-mile lollipop loop

Difficulty: Easy; moderate up stairs

Hiking time: About 2 hours

Start: At the south end of the Lake Chinnabee Recreation Area parking lot

Trail surface: Short section of pavement, dirt and rock footpath

Best seasons: Year-round; open sunrise–sunset

Canine compatibility: Dogs permitted; leash required

Fees and permits: Day-use fee

County: Clay

Land status: National forest

Trail contact: Talladega National Forest, Talladega Ranger District, 1001 North St., Hwy. 21 N., Talladega, AL 35160; (256) 362-2909; www.fs.usda.gov/detail/alabama/about-forest/districts/?cid=fsbdev3_002555

Maps: DeLorme: Alabama Atlas & Gazetteer: Page 32, F5

Special considerations: Flash flooding is possible along the banks of Cheaha Creek and Lake Chinnabee. The lower pools you'll pass at mile 0.4 can be crowded in summer, so plan to arrive early. The Lake Chinnabee Recreation Area is closed from Oct to Mar 1.

Finding the trailhead: From Lineville at the intersection of AL 9 and AL 49, take AL 49 north 14.2 miles. Turn left onto AL 281 South. Travel 4.9 miles (passing Cheaha State Park on the way) and turn right onto Cheaha Road. Travel 3.6 miles and turn left onto Lake Chinnabee Road. In 1.3 miles arrive at the Lake Chinnabee Recreation Area. The trailhead and parking will be on your left. Trailhead GPS: N33 27.594' / W85 52.433'; Devils Den GPS: N33 27.379' / W85 52.200'; Spillway GPS: N33 27.778' / W85 52.686'

The Hike

The southernmost mountains of the Appalachians do not disappoint on this 3.3-mile hike to Devils Den. The "den" is a narrow gorge where the water of Cheaha Creek rushes down its boulder-strewn channel as it makes its way to Lake Chinnabee, which is where we begin this hike.

Devil's Den as seen from the elevated walkway on the Chinnabee Silent Trail.

We will be using two trails for this hike—the Chinnabee Silent Trail and the Lakeshore Loop, which will lead us to a great view of a CCC dam. More on that in a moment.

The trail meanders along the banks of Cheaha Creek where you will be treated to the soothing sounds of the rushing water. At just about a half mile into the trip, you will arrive at the impressive multi-tiered cascades of Devils Den. There is a wonderful swimming hole here that is refreshing in the hot southern summer, but be warned—it gets crowded. Plan to arrive early.

From there, continue heading south and soon you will find yourself climbing some stone steps carved into the rock, which culminate in a wooden walkway and rock footpath. Look around and you will see the entire length of Devils Den Gorge back to the north, an amazing sight any time of year but especially in autumn when

Hikers call it Alabama's most scenic trail, the Chinnabee Silent Trail. Thousands hike it each year, but few know the story of how it came to be and that unique name.

It all began in 1962 when a group of Boy Scouts from the Alabama Institute for Deaf and Blind made a commitment to give back to the community. Scouting had been an important part of the school since 1934, where the boys were taught valuable life lessons and an appreciation of the outdoors.

In that year the school's Troop 29, all of whom were deaf, began working with the US Forest Service, volunteer trail builders, and fellow Scouts to create many of the trails that wind through the forest.

In early 1970 the troop's leader, Moran Colburn (who was also deaf) decided that the Scouts should build their own trail. On April 11, 1973, Troop 29 reached an agreement with the US Forest Service to begin work on the new path, a path that would connect Lake Chinnabee at the base of the state's highest mountain, Cheaha, to the Odum Scout Trail.

Armed with pickaxes and hoes, the boys began doing the hard work of cutting a 24-inch-wide hiking trail into the steep, sloping, rocky mountainside, digging out roots, and assisting in building wooden walkways—backbreaking work to say the least.

It took almost eighty Boy Scouts two years to complete the trail, but what a trail, following the banks of Cheaha Creek with its many swift shoals and cascades, taking in the breathtaking Cheaha Falls, and that incredible stone and wooden platform that clings to a cliff giving you spectacular views of Devils Den Gorge.

The trail was named for Creek Indian chief Selocta Chinnabee, an ally of General Andrew Jackson during the Creek Indian Wars. The "Silent" part of the name pays homage to the Scouts who made the trail a reality.

Devils Den and Lake Chinnabee Spillway, Cheaha Falls

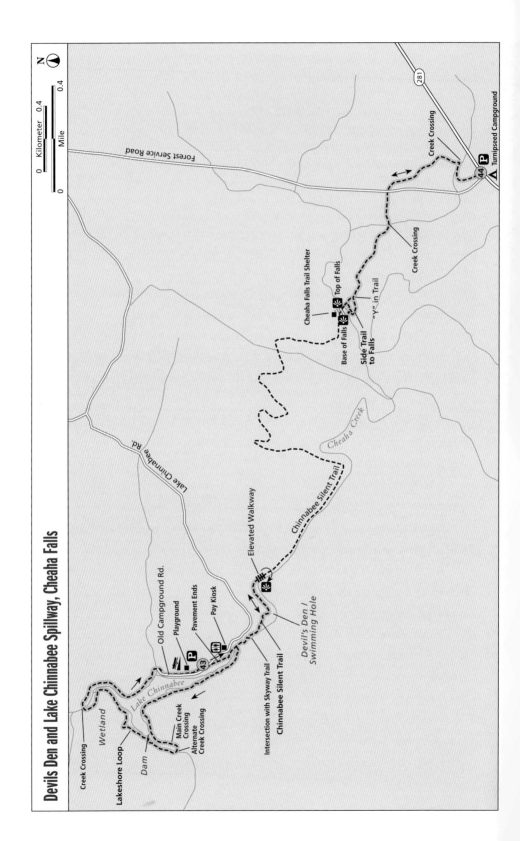

Your first glimpse of the CCC dam on the Lakeshore Loop.

the fiery gold, orange, and red leaves frame the picture and the rush of water churns down the channel.

After visiting the falls, head back the way you came and then hike around the lake itself on the Lakeshore Loop trail to see the handiwork of the CCC from the 1930s—a multi-step quartzite dam that impounds the water of Cheaha Creek. The dark staircase waterfall is illuminated with the glistening lake water as it pours over the spillway. The trail is especially nice from spring to late summer when wildflowers border the path and frog song serenades you. It is more overgrown than most paths in the forest, and the path along the west side of the lake is narrow with a drop to the lake, so use caution.

See Miles and Directions for options including a fun overnight trip.

Miles and Directions

0.0 Start from the south end of the parking lot and head south on the paved walkway. In a few yards you will pass a restroom on the left where the pavement ends. This is the start of the Chinnabee Silent Trail.

0.2 Continue straight to the southeast, passing the turn for the Lakeshore Loop.

0.3 Continue straight, passing the intersection with the Skyway Loop Trail on the right. Along this stretch there are many drops, cascades, and swimming holes.

0.4 Begin to see the impressive series of drops, cascades, and swimming holes of Devils Den.

0.5 Start climbing up a rock wall on a series of stone steps.

0.6 You'll find yourself walking on a wooden gangway along the side of the cliff. At the top, arrive at a spectacular view of Devils Den Gorge from the walkway. When ready, turn around and retrace your steps to mile 0.2.

1.2 Back at the intersection with the Lakeshore Loop, turn left (west). You will have to ford the creek, which could be running swiftly. Use caution and pick your best way. On the other side, the trail turns right (northwest) to follow the banks of the lake.

1.7 Pass a bench on the right.

1.8 Arrive at the south side of the dam. Continue following the trail to the southwest.

1.9 Supposedly this is where you cross the flow from the dam, but many times it is too fast and deep. I found an easier crossing by continuing south a few yards. Carefully pick your way across the creek to the west. Once on the other side, turn right and continue on the trail to the north.

2.1 Pass the dam once again to your right.

2.3 Pass a bench next to the lake.

2.4 Ford a small feeder stream and cross through a wetland over some footbridges.

2.5 Cross a narrow feeder creek over a footbridge.

2.7 Arrive at the Old Campground Road. Follow the paved roadway to the south, passing a boat ramp and playground on the way.

3.3 Arrive back at the trailhead.

Options: If you do not want to do the full hike described here, you can skip the hike around the lake for a 1.4-mile out-and-back walk. For a longer trek, you can continue on the Chinnabee Silent Trail past the gorge view at mile 0.6 to visit Cheaha Falls (hike 44), where you would turn around and retrace your steps to the trailhead for an out-and-back hike of 7.1 miles, or you could spend the night in the Cheaha Shelter with its breathtaking views of the mountains before returning the next day.

44 Cheaha Falls

Next to Devils Den (hike 43), Cheaha Falls is the most popular hike and waterfall in the Talladega National Forest because of its easy access and, more importantly, its sheer beauty as Cheaha Creek tumbles down rocky quartzite steps into a turquoise pool, the perfect spot to sit and reflect or maybe take a dip on a hot summer day. There is also an option to extend this hike into a longer day hike to Devils Den (see Miles and Directions).

See map on page 168.
Height of falls: 20 feet
Type of falls: Cascade
Distance: 2.3 miles out and back
Difficulty: Easy
Hiking time: About 1 hour
Start: Across the road to the north of the parking lot on AL 281, where you will see the trailhead to the right of a dirt forest service road
Trail surface: Dirt and rock footpath
Best seasons: Year-round; open sunrise–sunset
Canine compatibility: Dogs permitted; leash required

Fees and permits: None
County: Cleburne
Land status: National forest
Trail contact: Talladega National Forest, Talladega Ranger District, 1001 North St., Hwy. 21 N., Talladega, AL 35160; (256) 362-2909; www.fs.usda.gov/detail/alabama/about-forest/districts/?cid=fsbdev3_002555
Maps: DeLorme: Alabama Atlas & Gazetteer. Page 32, F5
Special considerations: None. Just have fun.

Finding the trailhead: From Lineville at the intersection of AL 49 and AL 9 (Main Street), take AL 9 west 200 feet and turn right onto 2nd Avenue North. In 200 feet, turn left onto Talladega Street. Travel 0.8 mile and turn right onto Highland Road. (In 1.6 miles Highland becomes Watershed Road then Highland again.) Travel 5.8 miles and turn left onto Clairmont Springs Road. Travel 2.3 miles and turn right onto Blue Ridge Road. Continue on Blue Ridge 2.7 miles and turn right onto Adams Gap Road/AL 281. The parking lot will be on the right in 3.7 miles. Trailhead GPS: N33 26.672' / W85 50.487'; Falls GPS: N33 27.116' / W85 51.025'

The Hike

As mentioned in our previous hike to Devils Den (hike 43), in 1973 a group of Boy Scouts from Troop 29 of the Alabama Institute for Deaf and Blind began building one of the premier hiking trails in the Talladega National Forest, the Chinnabee Silent Trail. The trail was completed in 1976 and is the most popular and arguably the most beautiful in the forest.

The two highlights of the trail are the spectacular gorge and falls that I described in the Devils Den hike, which is located on the north end of the trail, and the waterfall we will visit on this trek, Cheaha Falls, on the south end of the path.

The dual plunge of Cheaha Falls is an open invitation to sit and relax the world away.

This is an easy 2.3-mile out-and-back hike that begins at the parking lot on AL 281. The trail is only vaguely blazed, but it is easy enough to follow the well-worn path.

The trail meanders through a hardwood forest, passing seasonal wildflowers like spring beauty, until it arrives at the top of the falls and its rushing waters, a favorite camping spot for backpackers. From here the path follows the rocky bluff to the south until at mile 1.1, a nondescript side trail winds its way downhill beneath a tall rock bluff and leads you to the bottom of the falls. The soothing, tumbling flow will have you lingering for quite a while, getting lost in the sparkling spray and calming roar before it's time to retrace your steps to the trailhead and civilization.

Much like the Devils Den hike, Cheaha Falls is easily accessible, which means in the summertime it can get crowded, so make plans to arrive early. As an added bonus, if you carefully cross the creek at the top of the falls and take a short 500-foot walk up the hill to the top of the ridge, you will come to the Cheaha Falls Shelter, a spacious trail shelter used by backpackers where you will get an expansive view of the Talladega Mountains.

If you would like a longer hike, there is an option to extend this hike into a 7.3-mile out-and-back that includes Devils Den (see the options under Miles and Directions) or a nice 17-mile overnight backpacking trek (see the sidebar).

Miles and Directions

0.0 Start at the Chinnabee Silent Trail parking area on AL 281. Cautiously cross the highway on an angle to the north to the well-marked trailhead. It is to the right of an intersecting forest service road.

0.2 Cross a creek to the north.

0.5 Cross a forest service road to the west, picking up the trail on the opposite side.

0.7 Cross a second creek

1.0 Come to a Y in the trail. Take the right fork to the northwest to see the top of the falls. When done viewing, turn left (south). Use caution along the steep rock bluff.

1.1 A side trail heads downhill to the bottom of the falls, following a tall rock bluff.

1.2 Arrive at the base of the falls. When ready, turn around and head back up to the top of the bluff, but instead of turning left, continue straight to the southeast.

1.3 Back at the Y from mile 1.0, turn right (southwest) and retrace your steps to the trailhead.

2.3 Arrive back at the parking lot.

Option: For a longer 7.3-mile out-and-back trek, cross the creek at the top of Cheaha Falls and continue on the Chinnabee Silent Trail to see the mountain views at the Cheaha Trail Shelter, then continue on to visit Devil's Den (hike 43), where you will turn around and return to the trailhead.

Looking for a great overnight backpacking trip? Try this hike that combines three famous Talladega trails to complete a 17-mile-long loop. Start at the Devils Den (hike 43) trailhead and hike the Chinnabee Silent Trail to Cheaha Falls where you can spend the night in the trail shelter with beautiful mountain views. From here, continue south on the Chinnabee all the way to the Turnipseed parking area (the trailhead for Cheaha Falls, hike 44), where the trail intersects with the Pinhoti Trail. Take the Pinhoti Trail to the Skyway Loop Trail with more mountain views, which will take you back to Lake Chinnabee and the trailhead. Find out more on the Talladega National Forest website (see Trail contacts).

45 Boulder Canyon

This amazing little 1-mile loop hike is tucked away in the woods of Vestavia Hills near an elementary school, but what it lacks in length is made up for with the many cascades that tumble down short rock bluffs and rocky boulder-strewn channels, hence the name Boulder Canyon. The falls range from short 3-foot drops to a couple of 6-foot cascades and the grand finale, a 15-foot plunge falls at the end of the hike.

Height of falls: Various—tallest 15 feet
Type of falls: Cascade
Distance: 1.0-mile loop
Difficulty: Easy
Hiking time: About 1 hour
Start: At the trailhead to the north of the parking lot through a wooden fence
Trail surface: Narrow dirt and rock footpath
Best seasons: Sept–Apr; open sunrise–sunset
Canine compatibility: Dogs permitted; leash required
Fees and permits: None
County: Jefferson

Land status: City school property/city park
Trail contact: Vestavia Hills Parks and Recreation, 1289 Montgomery Hwy., Vestavia Hills, AL 35216; (205) 978-0166; vhal.org/departments/parks-recreation/facilities/; Vestavia Hills City Schools, 1204 Montgomery Hwy., Montevallo, AL 35216; (205) 402-5134; www.vestavia.k12.al.us/
Maps: *DeLorme: Alabama Atlas & Gazetteer.* Page 31, F6
Special considerations: Do not hike the trail while school is in session.

Finding the trailhead: From Birmingham start at the intersection of I-20 and I-65. Take I-65 south 8.2 miles. Take exit 252 (US 31) and turn left onto US 31 North. Take US 31 north 1.3 miles and turn right onto Vestridge Drive. Travel 0.2 mile and continue straight on Badham Drive. Travel 0.4 mile and turn left onto Willoughby Road. In less than 0.1 mile, turn left onto Merry Fox Lane. The parking lot and trailhead will be on the left in 0.1 mile. Trailhead GPS: N33 25.708' / W86 47.183'; Falls GPS: scattered throughout the hike

The Hike

The trail begins to the north across the street from the parking lot on Merry Fox Lane. Throughout the hike, the path is a root- and rock-strewn dirt trail.

There really isn't a right or wrong way to hike Boulder Canyon. The trails meander around the property, interconnecting to give you nice views of several drops and cascades, including one beautiful long cascade that tumbles over its boulder-strewn channel for some 200 feet from end to end. The hike culminates with the main waterfall—a 15-foot plunge near the school.

While the hike is suitable for older children, there are some very narrow sections with pretty steep drops. If you have small children, you may want to consider doing

The grand finale of the Boulder Canyon loop hike. ▶

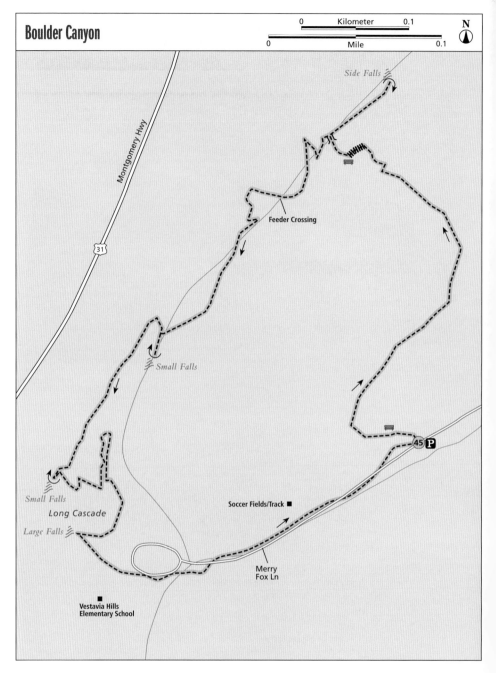

0 — Kilometer — 0.1

0 — Mile — 0.1

N

Side Falls

Montgomery Hwy

31

Feeder Crossing

Small Falls

Small Falls

Long Cascade

Large Falls

45 P

Soccer Fields/Track ■

Merry
Fox Ln

■
Vestavia Hills
Elementary School

a shorter 0.6-mile out-and-back walk by reversing the directions below, starting at the end of the hike and passing the main falls at the school before visiting the long cascade at mile 0.7, where you will turn around and head back to the parking area.

You will have a few short climbs up and down some hills using railroad tie stairs. These stairs have rope handrails next to them to help you down. The ties are held in

The trail at Boulder Canyon winds around a swift creek that forms several waterfalls.

place with rebar, and in some cases those steel bars stick up an inch or two above the wood. Watch your step so you don't trip or step on them.

Miles and Directions

0.0 Start at the trailhead across the street to the north from the parking lot. In less than 0.1 mile, come to a Y intersection with a tree in the middle of the fork. Take the right fork to the northeast.

0.2 Come to an intersection. Continue straight to the northwest. In less than 0.1 mile, pass a bench on the left and head steeply downhill toward the creek using railroad tie stairs.

0.3 Come to the creek and a bridge. A short side trail on each side of the bridge invites you to turn right and head upstream 100 feet to explore the first falls. When ready, cross the bridge and head left (southwest).

0.4 Come to a Y intersection. Take the right fork to the northwest and come to the second tiered falls. Cross the stream over the rocky bed of the feeder to the west, where it then turns left and returns to follow the creek to the north.

0.5 View another small falls on the left.

0.7 A nondescript trail comes in from the right. Take the trail down the railroad tie steps to the falls below. You will be in the middle of the long cascade. When ready, head back up the stairs and turn right (southeast) to continue on the trail.

0.8 Take the short side trail to the right (west) that leads you to the main waterfall. When ready, turn left and head southeast toward the school.

0.9 Cross a wooden footbridge and you will be in the cul-de-sac of the school parking lot. Follow Merry Fox Lane to the east, passing a playground and soccer field on your left.

1.0 Arrive back at the trailhead.

46 Moss Rock Preserve

Not one, not two, but five waterfalls tumble down the sandstone ledges and boulders of Moss Rock Preserve. This 4.9-mile-long route weaves its way through the preserve, leading you to unique and rare plants in a sandstone glade, beautiful (and fun) geologic features, and, of course, the relaxing sounds of its many seasonal waterfalls.

Height of falls: Various, tallest about 20 feet
Type of falls: Cascade
Distance: 4.9 miles out and back with center loop
Difficulty: Moderate
Hiking time: About 2 hours
Start: At the trailhead on the east side of the parking lot through the split-rail fence
Trail surface: Dirt with rocks
Best seasons: Sept–June; open sunrise–sunset
Canine compatibility: Dogs permitted; leash required
Fees and permits: None
County: Jefferson

Land status: City park
Trail contact: City of Hoover Parks and Recreation, Hoover City Hall, 100 Municipal Ln., Hoover, AL 35216; (251) 444-7500; www .hooveral.org/214/Moss-Rock-Preserve
Maps: *DeLorme: Alabama Atlas & Gazetteer:* Page 30, F5; additional trail maps available on the preserve's website
Special considerations: The sandstone glade you will visit is a very fragile landscape that is easily killed off if walked on. If you find yourself off trail and on the glade, please be careful to only step on rocks.

Finding the trailhead: From Hoover, start at the intersection of I-65 and US 31 at exit 252. Take US 31 south for 1.3 miles. Turn right onto Patton Chapel Road and travel 2 miles. Turn left onto Preserve Parkway. Travel 0.5 mile and turn right to stay on Preserve Parkway. In 0.2 mile, continue straight at the traffic circle to stay on Preserve Parkway. In 1.1 miles turn right onto Sulphur Springs Road; the trailhead will be on the right in 0.1 mile. Trailhead GPS: N33 22.579' / W86 51.196'; Falls GPS: scattered throughout the hike

The Hike

Moss Rock Preserve is a unique greenspace, an oasis located in the middle of an upscale neighborhood, but you will feel miles away from civilization as you wind your way along this 4.9-mile-long route that weaves its way through 349 acres of hickory, sweetgum, flowering dogwood, Florida maple, and southern red oak forested hillsides; crisscrosses the clear, cool waters of Hurricane Creek; and leads you to unique and rare plants in a sandstone glade and, of course, its many waterfalls.

While generally short in height (the tallest being about 20 feet tall), what they lack in size they make up for in the sheer number of them. Remember, though, that the waterfalls at Moss Rock are seasonal and could be nonexistent in the hot southern summers.

One of many cascades that dot the landscape of Moss Rock Preserve.

There are many trails that crisscross the preserve, all interconnected to provide countless loop treks. The route I have chosen here will allow you to explore all the waterfalls found at Moss Rock using a combination of three trails—the Blue, White, and Orange, so named because that is the color each of these trails have been blazed. Intersections are easy to navigate, with numbered signs on posts that tell the direction and mileage to key features in the preserve.

The trail is rated moderate, but some may find the climbs up to the Upper Falls and Turtle Rock (which really does look like a giant sleeping turtle—Gamera?) a bit of a challenge. Locals call that climb the "Cardio Trail."

One of the more interesting waterfalls along this hike is Tunnel Falls, which disappears under the rocks to the north of the trail only to reappear just downhill.

What is a sandstone glade? A glade is an open area where bedrock is either at or just below the earth's surface. There is a very thin layer of soil on top, making it difficult for trees and plants to grow. Sandstone glades, with their slightly sloping and moon-like appearance, occur in only thirty-five places in the world, one of those being Moss Rock Preserve in Hoover. While larger species of plants and trees have a difficult time growing in this landscape, smaller and rarer plants, mosses, and lichens do take hold and thrive in this environment.

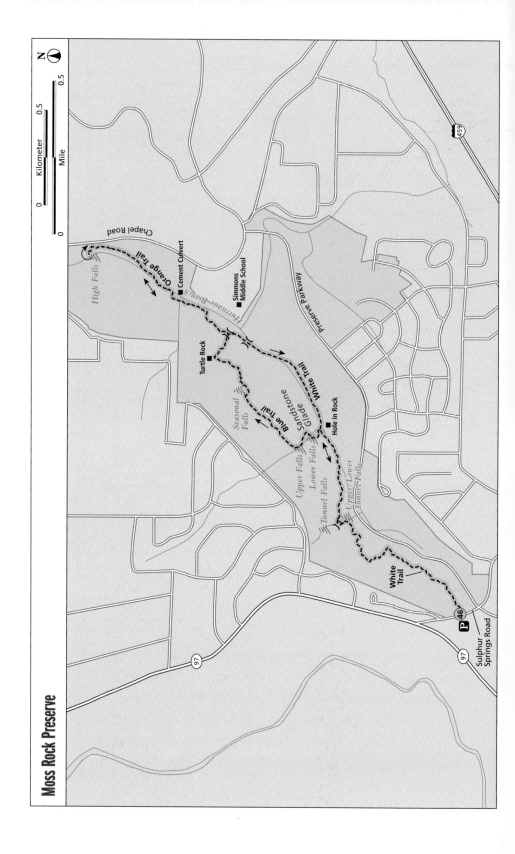

Moss Rock Preserve

Sure beats the playground at Chik-fil-A—a day climbing on Hole in Rock.

Miles and Directions

0.0 Start at the trailhead on the east side of the parking lot. In less than 0.1 mile, the trail turns right onto the Blue Trail. Arrive at Patriotic Junction where the Red, White, and Blue Trails intersect. Turn left (east) onto the White Trail.

0.8 Pass Lower Tunnel Falls on the right. Continue straight to the north and cross the creek over a bridge to the east. Upper Tunnel Falls will be on your left as you cross.

0.9 Crossing a bridge over Hurricane Creek, there is a small cascade on the left.

1.1 Cross the creek over a bridge to the north then turn right and in a few yards you will come to Lower Falls. When done viewing, return to the bridge but do not cross it. Instead, head north on the Blue Trail toward Upper Falls.

1.2 Arrive at the Sandstone Glade. The trail continues to the north.

1.4 Pass a small seasonal cascade to the right. In less than 0.1 mile, arrive at Upper Falls. Topping out on the ridge, turn right (northeast) onto the Blue Trail.

1.7 A short side trail to the left (northwest) that leads to a small waterfall on the left. After visiting, return to the Blue Trail.

1.9 Arrive at Turtle Rock. Turn right (southeast) here to rejoin the White Trail.

2.1 Cross a bridge over Hurricane Creek then turn left (east) onto the Orange Trail.

2.2 Take the left fork of a Y to the northeast. Rock-hop your way across the creek and pick up the Orange Trail on the opposite side. Once across, the trail makes a sharp left turn.

2.5 Take the left fork of a very subtle Y intersection.

2.6 Scramble up some rocks next to the creek.

2.7 Arrive at High Falls. When ready, turn around and retrace your steps to the bridge at mile 2.1.

3.3 Back at the bridge, cross Hurricane Creek once again, then turn left onto the White Trail.

3.8 Arrive at Hole in Rock.

4.9 Arrive back at the trailhead.

47 Peavine Falls

The centerpiece of Oak Mountain State Park is the 65-foot-tall plunge waterfall known as Peavine Falls. The falls usually runs year-round, although late in the summer it can be only a trickle; visit fall through spring when you're sure to get a thundering show as the water churns white and the sound echoes down the gorge. The Falls Loop Trail will also take you down the gorge away from the falls alongside Peavine Branch, where you will have the opportunity to catch a second, smaller but beautiful cascade farther downstream.

Height of falls: 65 feet
Type of falls: Plunge
Distance: 1.8-mile loop
Difficulty: Moderate
Hiking time: 1–1.5 hours
Start: At the Green Trail trailhead on the northeast side of the parking lot at the kiosk
Trail surface: Dirt, rock, and root-strewn footpath, short section of gravel road, ford of Peavine Branch
Best seasons: Year-round; open 7 a.m.–8 p.m.
Canine compatibility: Dogs permitted; leash required
Fees and permits: Day-use fee
County: Shelby

Land status: State park
Trail contact: Oak Mountain State Park, 200 Terrace Dr., Pelham, AL 35124; (205) 620-2520; www.alapark.com/parks/oak-mountain-state-park
Maps: *DeLorme: Alabama Atlas & Gazetteer:* Page 31, H6; trail maps available at the camp store or on the park's website
Special considerations: Crowds flock to the falls usually beginning mid-morning, so get there early. Don't cross the stream at the base of the falls when it is high and fast flowing, and remember that the Green-White Connector may be too steep for smaller children (see Miles and Directions for options).

Finding the trailhead: From Pelham at the intersection of I-65 (exit 242) and CR 52, take CR 52 east 0.2 mile and turn left onto Oak Mountain Trail. Travel 0.5 mile and turn right to continue on Oak Mountain Trail for another 1.9 miles. Turn right onto CR 35. In 0.4 mile, CR 35 becomes John Findlay III Drive. Continue 2.1 miles and arrive at the entrance gate. Pay your day-use fee and continue on John Findlay III Drive another 2.1 miles. Turn right onto Terrace Drive. Travel 2.1 miles and turn left onto Peavine Falls Road (see note in text). Travel 3 miles and arrive at the parking area. The Green Trail trailhead is on the left (northeast) side of the parking lot. The road is narrow with tight bends going up to the trailhead. Watch for oncoming traffic and road cyclists. A couple of mountain bike trails also cross the road. Yield to crossing bikes. The parking lot is very large with plenty of room for the crowds that visit. Trailhead GPS: N33 18.159' / W86 45.749'; Falls GPS: N33 18.344' / W86 45.384'

The Hike

Peavine Falls is located just south of Birmingham in Oak Mountain State Park and is rightfully the centerpiece of the park. The 65-foot waterfall is amazing when there is

Peavine Falls roars into its gorge at Oak Mountain State Park.

a good flow in the stream. A powerful wall of water plunges down the craggy rocks, crashing to the bottom, its roar echoing down the narrow gorge.

There are a couple of bonus waterfalls on this hike as well. After climbing steeply down off a ridge to meet up with Peavine Branch, you will cross the stream over a footbridge, and when the water is really flowing, another cascade—about 50 feet in length—tumbles down the hillside to your right.

Later, after arriving at the base of Peavine Falls, you will head downstream where you will come to yet another smaller cascade, this one with a long slide in the center of it. The loop ends at the White Trail trailhead on the opposite side of the parking lot from where you started.

This hike uses seven trails to complete the loop—the Green, Green-White Connector, White, Blue, Falls Creek Trail, Falls Loop, and Peavine Falls Trails. All trails in the park are well blazed with dollar bill–size metal markers that are the color of the trail you're on—green for the Green Trail, green and white for the Green-White

The calm before the storm—the trail parallels Peavine Creek before thundering down into the gorge.

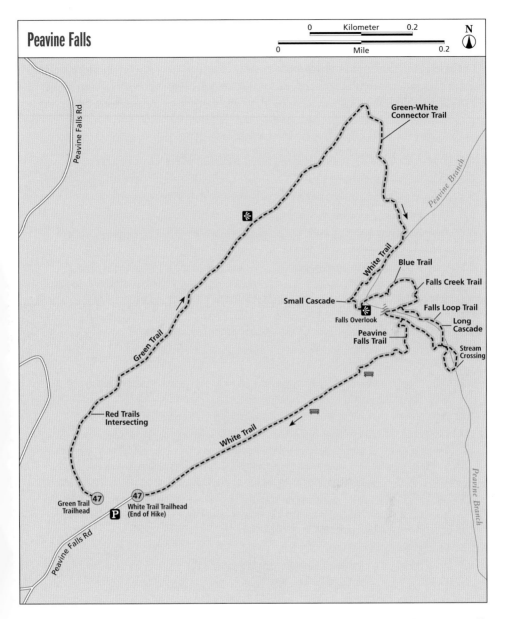

Peavine Falls

Kilometer

Mile

N

Peavine Falls Rd

Green-White
Connector Trail

Peavine Branch

White Trail

Blue Trail

Falls Creek Trail

Small Cascade

Falls Loop Trail

Falls Overlook

Long
Cascade

Peavine
Falls Trail

Stream
Crossing

Green Trail

Red Trails
Intersecting

White Trail

Green Trail
Trailhead

47

47

White Trail Trailhead
(End of Hike)

P

Peavine Falls Rd

Peavine Branch

Connector, and so on. The only exceptions are on the Falls Loop and Peavine Falls Trails, which use white diamond metal markers.

The trails also have a series of colored and numbered 4-by-4-inch poles. The colors represent the trail you are on, and the numbers are markers so that in the event of an emergency, you can contact authorities to get help and let them know exactly where you are.

Once you visit Peavine and head downstream to view the second, smaller cascade, it's time to get your feet wet. There is no right or wrong way to cross the stream, but when the water is deep and swiftly flowing, you should consider doing the option listed in Miles and Directions for your own safety.

Remember that the trip down from the first ridge to the falls is very steep. Take that into consideration if the stream is too swift to cross. You will have to climb back out and it's rather difficult. Again, refer to Miles and Directions for an alternate option.

Miles and Directions

0.0 Start at the Green Trail trailhead located on the northeast side of the parking lot.

0.1 Pass the Red Trail on the left.

0.4 Arrive at the top of the ridge and a short side trail on the right with an overlook.

0.6 Turn right (south) and head very steeply downhill on the Green-White Connector Trail.

0.8 Arrive at Peavine Branch. Turn right (southwest) onto the White Trail, which follows alongside the creek.

0.9 Cross a 30-foot-long footbridge over the creek and pick up the Blue Trail on the opposite side. When water is flowing, there is a nice 50-foot-long sliding cascade off to your right. In less than 0.1 mile, come to a Y in the trail. Take the left fork to the northeast to continue on the Blue Trail.

1.0 Turn right (south) onto the Falls Creek Trail and begin a serious downhill climb.

1.1 Arrive at the base of the falls. When done exploring, turn left (southeast) and follow the bank of the creek. This is the Falls Loop Trail.

1.2 Climb a set of stone stairs up a little hill. A really nice lower cascade begins here with a wide slide in the middle.

1.3 Pick your way carefully across the stream and pick up the loop trail on the other side.

1.4 Arrive once again at the base of the falls. When done exploring, turn right (south) away from the stream and head steeply uphill to the south on the Peavine Falls Trail. In less than 0.1 mile, arrive at Falls Overlook. Do not continue straight uphill from here. Turn left (south) and follow the trail as it switchbacks to the top of the ridge.

1.5 Top out on the rim of the gorge. Turn right (west) to continue on the Peavine Falls Trail. In less than 0.1 mile, arrive at the White Trail—a wide gravel road with benches on both sides. Head straight to the southwest on the White Trail.

1.6 Pass benches on both sides of the trail.

1.8 Arrive back at the parking lot and the White Trail trailhead.

Option: For an easier trek that's a little less steep and better for smaller kids—or if you can't ford the creek because it's too dangerous—do a 1-mile out-and-back by starting at the end of this hike on the White Trail and reverse the above directions from mile 1.8 to mile 1.3 so you can see both Peavine Falls and the lower cascade, then retrace your steps to the start.

48 Falling Rock Falls

Just south of Birmingham in the town of Montevallo, there is a little-known wildlife management area where a leisurely walk down a gravel road, past new-growth pines and an oil drilling rig, leads you to a hidden surprise that only locals know about—a tall, rocky bluff and a 90-foot plunge falls known as Falling Rock Falls.

Height of falls: 90 feet
Type of falls: Plunge
Distance: 1.8 miles out and back
Difficulty: Moderate
Hiking time: About 1 hour
Start: At the trailhead behind a steel gate on the north side west end of the parking area
Trail surface: Gravel road, dirt and rock footpath
Best seasons: Sept–May; open sunrise–sunset
Canine compatibility: Dogs permitted; leash required

Fees and permits: None
County: Shelby
Land status: Wildlife management area
Trail contact: Calera Gas Co. LLC, Eddings Town Rd., Montevallo, AL 35115; (205) 665-0322; www.caleragas.com
Maps: *DeLorme: Alabama Atlas & Gazetteer.* Page 37, B6
Special considerations: At Eddings Creek, you are at the top of the falls. The drop-off at the edge can be deceiving and can sneak up on you, so use caution.

Finding the trailhead: From Montevallo, at the intersection of College Drive and Middle Street, head northwest on Middle Street 0.6 mile and turn right onto CR 17. Travel 3.2 miles and turn left onto CR 22 West. Travel 2.3 miles; the dirt and gravel pull-off for parking will be on the right, with room for 15 cars comfortably and plenty of space to pull far enough away from the road. Do not park in front of the steel gate at the trailhead since machinery uses this entrance. Trailhead GPS: N33 09.952' / W86 53.960'; Falls GPS: N33 10.454' / W86 54.417'

The Hike

This 90-foot gem of a waterfall with its deep rock shelter is found at the Lanier Wildlife Management Area in Montevallo. The ribbon of water from Eddings Creek courses over the rocky ledge, forming a nice shallow pool below.

The falls have been a gathering spot for locals for many years, but more and more people are discovering it. The only drawback to this magnificent flow is that, unfortunately, some who visit believe that the walls of the rock shelter were put there to display their personal "artwork."

The unmarked trail begins to the north of the dirt and gravel pull-off on CR 22. Walk around the right side of the steel gate and head north on the wide gravel road. Three-quarters of this hike are on these roads, but don't worry. You will have a chance to duck into the woods in a bit.

You will come to three Ys in the road. At the second one at mile 0.5, you will pass a pretty little wetland on the left. Later, at the third Y where you take the right fork,

The 90-foot Falling Rock Falls draws its curtain across a deep rock shelter.

Falling Rock Falls

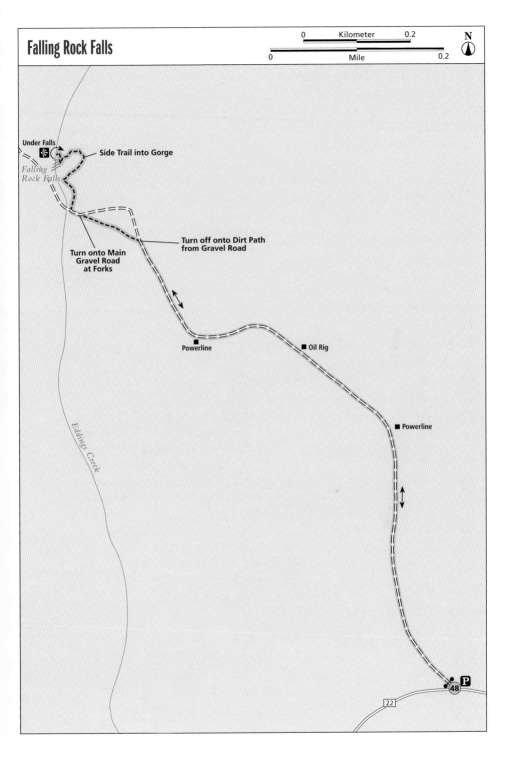

Under Falls

Side Trail into Gorge

Falling Rock Falls

Turn off onto Dirt Path from Gravel Road

Turn onto Main Gravel Road at Forks

Powerline

Oil Rig

Powerline

Eddings Creek

48

P

22

you will pass yet another little wetland where you will be serenaded by frog song after a good rain.

Eventually, you will leave the gravel road at mile 0.7 and come to a 4-foot-wide side trail into the woods on the left. The short dirt footpath soon becomes a wide clay and rock path (it's actually a runoff channel). Be careful along this section. The flat rocks can be slick during and after rain.

Once you arrive at Eddings Creek you will be at the top of the falls. Use caution when exploring. The edge and drop-off can be deceiving. The path from here is not well defined, but it is to your right and follows the rim of the gorge where you will get your first look at the falls through the trees. From here, there is a nondescript trail on the left that heads steeply down into the gorge using switchbacks and ends at the base of the falls.

Miles and Directions

0.0 Start at the steel gate by walking around the gate on the right side.

0.1 Cross under powerlines.

0.2 Cross under powerlines.

0.3 The road forks. Take the left fork to the northwest.

0.4 Pass an oil rig on the right.

0.6 Take the right fork in the road to the northwest.

0.7 Turn off the road onto a narrow, un-blazed dirt path into the woods on the left.

0.8 The trail widens out and is flat rock. Use caution when there is water running down its face. In less than 0.1 mile, turn right onto a narrow dirt and rock path. In a few yards, arrive at the top of the falls. Continue on the narrow footpath along the gorge rim to the right (north).

0.9 Carefully take a nondescript trail to the left and begin heading steeply down into the gorge. In less than 0.1 mile, arrive at the base of the falls and the rock shelter. When ready, turn around and retrace your steps to the trailhead.

1.8 Arrive back at the trailhead.

Central Alabama Honorable Mentions

M. Rocky Creek Waterfall

We'll return to the Pinhoti Trail and a spur off the famous long path, called the Heflin Spur, to visit a nice 20-foot cascade that is formed by a long since abandoned dam—the Rocky Creek Waterfall. The dam once generated energy for a power mill but was dismantled by Alabama Power back in 1926, leaving the dam to be hidden away in the thick forest of pine, white oak, sweet gum, and giant umbrella magnolia with its fragrant-blooming white flowers. The hike is 2.4 miles out and back and begins at the Heflin Spur trailhead on FS 500.

To find the trailhead, from the town of Heflin at the intersection of US 78 and CR 9, take US 78 west 2.7 miles, crossing under US 281. Turn right onto FS 500 and travel 0.2 mile. The well-marked gravel parking lot is on the right. Begin by heading east through the split-rail fence. For the first 0.5 mile, you will be walking the old Heflin to Oxford Road that was used to construct US 78 in the 1930s. This section runs parallel to a Norfolk Southern Railway line, so you may have a freight train running alongside. You will cross one creek along the way at mile 0.6, and then at mile 0.9, you will arrive at Rocky Branch. Turn left (north) here and hike up the creek bed 0.4 mile to the dam. Trailhead GPS: N33 38.935' / W85 37.887'; Falls GPS: N33 39.201' / W85 37.208'

South Alabama

Not all waterfalls in Alabama are found in the northern regions from Birmingham to Huntsville. In fact, there are a few that can actually be found far removed from the mountains of the north, in a region known as the "wiregrass."

The wiregrass is named for a long-stem variety of grass that grows in the region's longleaf pine forests. It is a relatively flat region where the terrain gently slopes southward toward the Gulf of Mexico, funneling the state's myriad streams and rivers down to the sea.

In this area the hard rock of the Piedmont region meets the sandy soils of the Coastal Plain, and where the two meet, there is a pretty substantial elevation difference—between 100 and 200 feet in some areas. This geologic line is known as a "fall line" and, of course, wherever a river or stream flows over this "line," there is a waterfall.

This fall line posed a real problem for transportation in the early development of south Alabama. Early passenger ships and barges could not navigate the many fast shoals and occasional waterfalls in the rivers, but those waterfalls would later be valuable to the region when they became an important source of power for the many mills that popped up along their banks.

For our journey to the waterfalls of Alabama, the south Alabama fall line that we're interested in stretches from Opelika to Montgomery. In the Auburn area, we will find four beautiful waterfalls. The first is a fun, educational trip for the entire family to view Hidden Falls (hike 49). Then we'll drive over to Chewacla State Park to see the handiwork of the Civilian Conservation Corps (CCC) from the 1930s and the spectacular cascade over the dam they built that forms Lake Chewacla, as well as a little-visited natural waterfall aptly named Natural Falls (hike 50). We will wrap up our journey to view the perfect example of what a fall line is by visiting "Satan's Garden," better known as Great Falls (hike 51).

The weather in the south region is subtropical, and late summer heat and humidity can make outdoor activities nearly impossible at times, so be sure to carry

The craftsmanship of the CCC from the 1930s is on display at Chewacla State Park.

plenty of water. The area's close proximity to the Gulf of Mexico means that the warm, moist Gulf air can produce brief but very heavy rainfall unexpectedly. In spring, temperatures range from daytime highs near 70°F to the mid-40s at night. The hot, humid summer gives way to great hiking weather from fall through winter, with temperatures averaging in the mid-50s in January with evening lows in the upper 30s.

For camping in the region near the waterfalls covered in this section, you can't beat Chewacla State Park. The park has preserved many of the buildings and landmarks created by the CCC in the 1930s (including the stone cabins) that give the park a rustic feel. There are plenty of improved and primitive tent campsites available, but be forewarned—the park gets very crowded in the fall when the Auburn Tigers football team has a home game. Plan your visit early. Learn more at www.alapark .com/parks/chewacla-state-park.

49 Hidden Falls

A fun and educational hike for the entire family awaits you just north of Auburn at the Kreher Preserve and Nature Center. Not only will you learn about birds, bees, and wildflowers through informational signage and displays, but you will also be treated to the aptly named star of the preserve—the 20-foot tiered cascade called Hidden Falls. It really is hidden and sneaks up on you.

Height of falls: 20 feet
Type of falls: Cascade
Distance: 1.6-mile loop
Difficulty: Easy
Hiking time: About 1 hour
Start: At the trailhead on the northeast side of the parking lot through the wooden fence
Trail surface: Some gravel path, mostly dirt
Best seasons: Sept–May; open sunrise–sunset
Canine compatibility: Dogs not allowed
Fees and permits: None
County: Lee
Land status: Auburn University–administered preserve

Trail contact: Kreher Preserve and Nature Center, 222 N. College St., Auburn, AL 36830; (334) 844-8091; www.wp.auburn.edu/preserve/?
Maps: DeLorme: Alabama Atlas & Gazetteer. Page 47, A6; a trail map is available to view on the kiosk at the trailhead
Special considerations: Dogs are not permitted in the preserve. The gorge that's formed by the creek at the falls is steep. Preserve managers ask that you stand behind the split-rail fence to view it and do not climb down to the bottom.

Finding the trailhead: From Auburn at the intersection of AL 14 and AL 147/Shug Jordan Parkway, head north on Shug Jordan Parkway 2.8 miles. Turn left onto AL 147 North/North College Street. Travel 1.6 miles and the parking lot will be on the right. The trailhead is on the northeast side of the gravel lot. Trailhead GPS: N32 39.597' / W85 29.261'; Falls GPS: N32 39.769' / W85 29.142'

The Hike

This is a great little hike that families will really enjoy through the Louise Kreher Preserve and Nature Center, which is operated by Auburn University. This small educational preserve has many exhibits along the park's trails that teach us a little history, and give us a chance to learn about snakes and raptors, view butterflies at a butterfly garden, even visit a live honeybee exhibit. And then there is that hidden secret—Hidden Falls.

Following the Hidden Falls Trail as we do for this hike, you will find yourself walking along the banks of a small creek wondering to yourself, "How could such a small brook create a decent waterfall?" Suddenly, there it is—the 20-foot cascade

From a small creek comes this gem of a waterfall—
Hidden Falls at the Kreher Nature Preserve in Auburn.

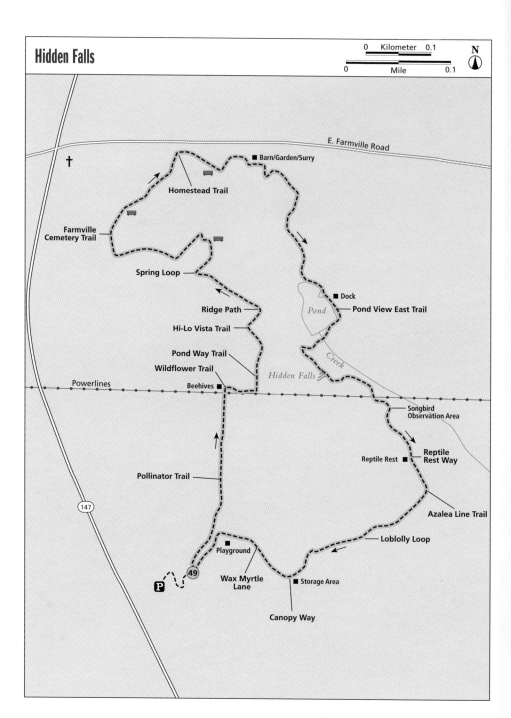

Hidden Falls

0 Kilometer 0.1

0 Mile 0.1

N

E. Farmville Road

Barn/Garden/Surry

Homestead Trail

Farmville Cemetery Trail

Spring Loop

Ridge Path

Hi-Lo Vista Trail

Pond Way Trail

Wildflower Trail

Powerlines

Beehives

Dock

Pond View East Trail

Pond

Creek

Hidden Falls

Songbird Observation Area

Reptile Rest Way

Reptile Rest

Azalea Line Trail

Pollinator Trail

147

Loblolly Loop

Playground

Wax Myrtle Lane

Storage Area

Canopy Way

P

49

cutting into the rock and dirt, forming a narrow gorge. To view the falls, the preserve asks that you stand behind the split-rail fence and don't climb down into the gorge. It's a good little drop to the bottom.

Our trip begins on the northeast side of the large, circular gravel parking lot through a tall wooden portal. There are any number of trails you can follow in the preserve, all of which interconnect in one way or another. We will use several different trails to make this loop, all of which use colored metal discs as markings, but there's little chance of getting lost on the well-worn paths. All intersections are well marked with wooden signs.

Miles and Directions

0.0 Start from the large wooden portal on the northeast side of the parking lot.

0.1 The Dead Timber Pass Trail comes in from the left at a private property sign in front of you. Continue to the north on the Pollinator Trail blazed with blue discs.

0.2 Cross under powerlines. Turn right onto the Wildflower Trail. A live beehive exhibit is right at the corner.

0.3 Turn left (north) onto the green-marked Pond Way Trail.

0.4 Turn left (northwest) onto the yellow-marked Ridge Path Trail. In less than 0.1 mile, turn right onto the Spring Loop Trail. In 30 feet, pass the remnants of an old moonshine still on the right.

0.5 Turn right (west) onto the Ridge Path Trail.

0.6 Turn right onto the blue-marked Farmville Cemetery Trail. In less than 0.1 mile, take the right fork onto the Boulder Ridge Trail.

0.7 Turn right (east) onto the blue-marked Homestead Trail.

0.8 Arrive at the old homestead barn. Continue past the barn and turn right (east) onto the Barn Trace/Pond Trail.

0.9 Cross the Pond Way Trail to the south and pick up the yellow-marked Pond View East Trail to Turtle Pond.

1.1 Turn right (southeastnorth) onto the Hidden Falls Trail. In less than 0.1 mile, you will arrive at Hidden Falls. When ready, from the observation boardwalk turn left (southeast) to continue on the Hidden Falls Trail.

1.2 Cross under the powerlines once again and pick up the Reptile Rest Way on the opposite side.

1.3 Turn right (southwest) onto the wide green-marked Azalea Line Trail.

1.5 Turn right onto the Canopy Trail to the northwest. In less than 0.1 mile, turn right (northwest) onto the dirt Wax Myrtle Lane. Back at the playground, turn left (southwest) and head to the trailhead.

1.6 Arrive back at the trailhead.

50 Natural Falls

Many people are familiar with the incredible stone waterfall created by the Civilian Conservation Corps (CCC) dam at Chewacla State Park, but there is yet another waterfall, this one a natural falls, just a short hike away from the dam that many people never visit but really need to—the 20-foot segmented waterfall known as Natural Falls, or Hidden Falls, or Gin Stone Hole. Take your pick of names, but don't miss this cascade when you visit the park.

Height of falls: CCC dam, 30 feet; Natural Falls, 20 feet
Type of falls: Cascade
Distance: 2.4-mile lollipop loop
Difficulty: Easy with only 1 small moderate climb at Natural Falls
Hiking time: About 1.5 hours
Start: On the east side of the parking lot through the opening in the wooden fence
Trail surface: Dirt, rock
Best seasons: Sept–May; open 8 a.m.–5 p.m.
Canine compatibility: Dogs permitted; leash required

Fees and permits: Day-use fee
County: Lee
Land status: State park
Trail contact: Chewacla State Park, 124 Shell Toomer Pkwy., Auburn, AL 36830; (334) 887-5621; www.alapark.com/parks/chewacla-state-park
Maps: *DeLorme: Alabama Atlas & Gazetteer.* Page 47, B6; trail maps available at the park entrance or on its website
Special considerations: Be aware that mountain bikes share the trail.

Finding the trailhead: From Auburn, at the intersection of AL 14 and AL 147/Shug Jordan Parkway, take Shug Jordan Parkway south 2.2 miles. Turn right onto AL 15 South/South College Street. Travel 1.7 miles and turn left onto CR 674/Shell Toomer Parkway. Travel 1.5 miles to continue straight into the park on Murphy Dr. Travel 0.3-mile and turn right into the trailhead parking area. Trailhead GPS: N32 33.173' / W85 28.599'; Falls GPS: Dam, N32 32.998' / W85 28.720'; Natural Falls, N32 32.757' / W85 29.129'

The Hike

Most people who visit Chewacla State Park gravitate to the CCC dam that blocks off Moore's Mill Creek and forms Lake Chewacla. It is a beautiful stepped spillway that flows most of the year with churning whitewater topping the dam. It is an easy walk to view the dam, but only a short hike past it there is another, less visited waterfall—Natural Falls.

Well, that's what Alabama State Parks calls it. If you look on Google Maps, you'll see that it's called "Hidden Falls." And if you talk to alumni from Auburn University,

Those who only go as far as the dam at Chewacla State Park are missing
a beautiful natural waterfall just a short distance down the trail.

The handiwork of the CCC is beautifully adorned with the turbulent flow from Lake Chewacla.

What historians call the greatest work program in history is on full display at Chewacla State Park. It was a program that not only provided jobs for thousands of young men during the depths of the Great Depression, but also left behind a legacy that still stands today—thousands of amazing national and state parks and forests across the country. These young men were part of the Civilian Conservation Corps (CCC).

Immediately after taking office in 1933, President Franklin D. Roosevelt enacted several new programs that would spur on the economy. One program, the CCC, became an army of young men that would bolster the nation's infrastructure as well as build exciting new places of recreation for the public.

At its height the CCC employed 500,000 men, all of them in their late teens to early twenties. These young men scoured the countryside building dams, state parks, and more. The men were provided food, shelter, clothing, and $30 a month in pay, $25 of which was sent home to their families.

Author and historian Robert Pasquill, in his book *The Civilian Conservation Corps in Alabama 1933-1942: A Great and Lasting Good*, says that the program employed 20,000 men in the state between 1933 and 1942, creating thirteen state forests and seven state parks.

they'll call it "Gin Stone Hole." I'm still not sure why they call it that. I'll get back with you.

The waterfall is found along a feeder of Chewacla Creek. It is a 20-foot segmented waterfall, but the impressive cascades, shoals, and shallow drops extend farther north a good 200 feet or so.

The park itself is 696 acres and was built by the Civilian Conservation Corps in 1935. There are over 15 miles of trails to hike and bike that circle the park's centerpiece, the 26-acre Lake Chewacla, and its feeder streams.

The hike to Natural Falls is a pleasant 2.4-mile lollipop loop through the mixed hardwood and pine forest. We'll be using four separate trails for this trek—the Lakeside Connector, Falls View, Creek View, and CCC Trails. The trails are not blazed but are well worn and easily discernable. There are a few jumbled intersections that may confuse you a bit. Just be on the lookout for the signage.

The hike begins at the hiker's parking lot off Murphy Drive where there are restrooms and a playground. You will begin your journey by following the banks of the lake southwestward on the Lakeside Connector. Along a hillside above the trail, you will see the incredible craftsmanship of the CCC in the impressive hand-cut stacked-stone cabins.

The trail wraps around the lake and ends at the CCC dam for incredible views of the water thundering over the spillway.

Continuing on to the southwest, the Falls View Trail meets up with the Creek View Trail where it switchbacks downhill, and soon you will see the fast shoals of the creek down below. At mile 1.3 there is a nondescript side trail that heads steeply downhill to view the main falls. Depending on the level of the creek, you can carefully clamber up the rocky creek bank to the north to view more shoals and drops. For the miles and directions described in this chapter, I chose to turn around after visiting the main falls and head back to the Creek View Trail because the creek was really high.

This is a pretty easy hike for all except the youngest of children but, as always, use caution with kids if you bring them, being careful on slippery rocks and near bluffs.

Also, while hiking any trail at Chewacla, be aware of your surroundings because mountain bikes share the routes. If you accidentally get off the trail route that is described here and onto another path, never fear. All intersections have directional signs back to the trailhead.

Oh, and one more thing. This can be a very busy park, and I mean very busy, especially during college football season when the Auburn Tigers have home games.

Miles and Directions

0.0 Start from the parking lot and head southwest through an opening in the split-rail fence downhill toward the lake. In a few yards, cross a boardwalk over a slough. Pick up the Lakeside Connector Trail on the opposite side. Turn left onto the trail and head southwest along the banks of the lake

Natural Falls

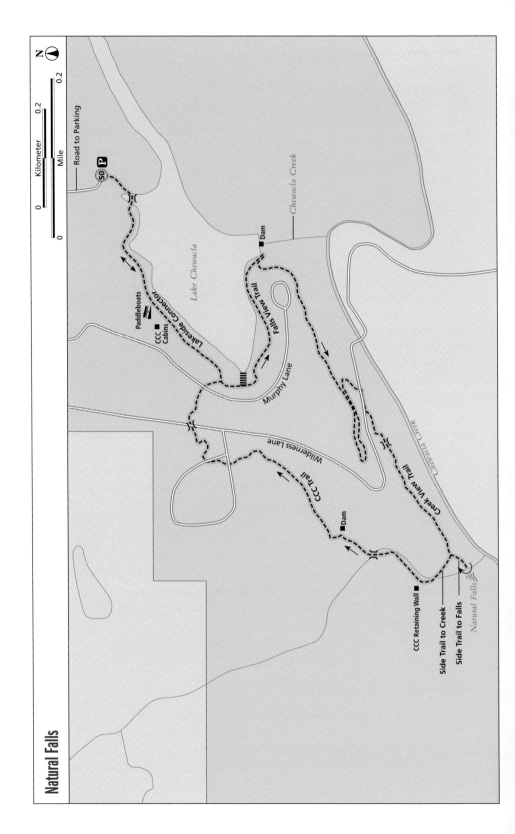

0.4 Come to the intersection of the Falls View and CCC Trails. Turn left (south) onto the Falls View Trail. In less than 0.1 mile, cross a 150-foot footbridge over a slough.

0.6 Arrive at the CCC dam to the left of a Y in the trail. The Falls View Trail continues on the right fork to the (south), but for now, take the left fork for a better view of the dam and falls. In less than 0.1 mile, after viewing the dam, turn around and return to the Y, then turn left (south) onto the Falls View Trail.

0.8 Come to a sign that points the direction to the trailhead (right) and Falls View Trail (straight ahead). Continue straight (southwest) on the Falls View Trail.

1.1 Come to a T intersection with an old dirt road. Turn right onto the dirt road, which is the start of the Creek View Trail. In less than 0.1 mile, come to a Y intersection. Take the left fork to the southwest. The trail is once again a narrow dirt footpath and is lined with moss- and lichen-covered rocks as it ducks back into the woods.

1.2 Cross a 30-foot bike bridge with wooden slats, nonskid strips, and wire mesh. You can see the creek and a fast shoal below on the left.

1.3 A narrow, nondescript side trail goes downhill to the creek and Natural Falls. This is the steepest descent of the loop.

1.4 Arrive at the base of Natural Falls. Depending on the level and speed of the creek, you can clamber up the rocky bank to the north to view more shoals and drops, but use caution on the slippery rocks. Turn around and retrace your steps to the Creek View Trail at mile 1.3, where you will turn left (northwest) onto the trail.

1.5 You can see the top of the falls and its fast shoals downhill on the left. In less than 0.1 mile, there is another nondescript trail on the left that leads to the creek. If you decide to head down, use caution, otherwise, continue straight to the north. In less than 0.1 mile pass a stone retaining wall that was built by the CCC in the 1930s.

1.6 Cross a 30-foot bridge. On the opposite side, continue to the north on the CCC Trail. In less than 0.1 mile, come to a T intersection. Turn right (northeast) to continue on the CCC Trail.

1.8 Come to a Y intersection with a sign for the CCC Trail to the left. Take the left fork to the north, crossing a dirt road and picking up the trail once again on the opposite side.

1.9 Come to a T intersection. Turn right (north) and head toward the trailhead on this short connector trail.

2.0 In less than 0.1 mile, cross a short 5-foot-long bridge and continue straight across a dirt road to the southeast. In less than 0.1 mile, come to a sign that reads "Trailhead" and points to the left. Turn left (northeast) and you are back on the Lakeside Connector Trail. Retrace your steps to the trailhead.

2.4 Arrive back at the trailhead.

51 Great Falls

The final hike in this book is a short roadside hike of only 0.1 mile down a gravel and rock path to the banks of Uchee Creek near Auburn. It might be a short hike, but wait until you see what awaits you—the thundering sound and power of a 40-foot-tall, 200-foot-wide block falls known as Great Falls, aka "Satan's Garden" to kayakers who often test their skills here.

Height of falls: 40 feet
Type of falls: Block
Distance: 0.1 mile out and back
Difficulty: Easy
Hiking time: About 5 minutes
Start: At the trailhead on the east side of the parking lot through the wooden fence
Trail surface: Gravel, dirt with rocks
Best seasons: Year-round; open sunrise-sunset
Canine compatibility: Dogs permitted; leash required

Fees and permits: None
County: Lee
Land status: County property
Trail contact: None
Maps: *DeLorme: Alabama Atlas & Gazetteer.* Page 47, E9
Special considerations: There is a steep bluff to view the falls from. Use caution. Do not attempt to drive down the gravel path that leads to the falls.

Finding the trailhead: From Opelika, at the intersection of I-85 (exit 60) and AL 51/Marvyn Parkway, take AL 51/Marvyn Parkway south 0.5 mile and turn left onto AL 169 South/Crawford Road. Travel 14.4 miles and turn right onto CR 206 (in 10.6 miles, the road name changes to CR 240). In 0.1 mile the very narrow gravel pull-off for parking will be on the left, with room for 2, maybe 3, cars to park parallel to the road. There is a slight grade downhill away from the road, so don't pull off too far. The trail is a gravel road to the top of the bluff. Do not drive it! It is a steep, rutted grade with a sheer drop-off to the bottom at the end. Trailhead GPS: N32 30.489' / W85 11.093'; Falls GPS: N32 30.511' / W85 11.084'

The Hike

Great Falls is the perfect example of what a fall line is—that area where two differing geologic regions (in this case the Piedmont and Coastal Plain) meet and a significant drop in the ground occurs. Wherever rivers and streams flow over a fall line, you have a waterfall.

The hike is a very short 0.1-mile out-and-back hike. In fact, you can see the falls from your car as you park on the side of the road. But take the walk down to the bluff above the creek for impressive views.

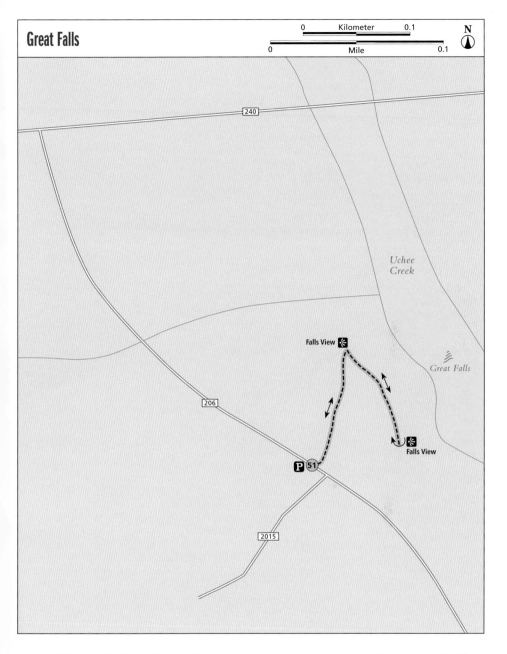

Great Falls

Uchee
Creek

Great Falls

Falls View

Falls View

206

240

2015

The trail is basically an old, rutted gravel road that starts right at the pull-off on CR 206 where you park, but don't try to drive down it! That could be fatal. Once you reach the bluff at the end of the road, a short side footpath takes you a bit farther south for a better view but, as always, use caution. The bluff is high and steep, the bottom not forgiving.

The perfect example of a fall line can be seen at Great Falls near Auburn.

Appendix A: Camping in the National Forests of Alabama

Many of the hikes in *Hiking Waterfalls Alabama* are located in the areas that have been designated as national forests and wilderness areas in the state (the Bankhead and Talladega National Forests and Sipsey and Cheaha Wildernesses). Hikers and backpackers can pitch a tent or hammock just about anywhere free of charge in these areas, what the forest service calls "dispersed camping," but you must follow these simple rules and regulations:

- Be self-contained: That means there are no amenities like trash disposal or restrooms.
- You can camp in an area for up to sixteen days but must move at least 5 miles after those sixteen days.
- There are many established campsites along the trails (those that hikers have already built with fire rings). Use those if you can to avoid creating a new campsite and disturbing vegetation and wildlife
- Camp on bare soil if possible, to avoid damage or killing plants and grass.
- Do not camp in the middle of a clearing or meadow; try to make your campsite less visible so that other visitors will see a "wild" setting.
- Do not try to level or dig trenches in the ground at your campsite. Pick a tent site that is already level with good drainage.
- Keep a pack-in, pack-out camp. Follow Leave No Trace guidelines.
- Contact the local US Forest Service office to see if any restrictions, especially fire restrictions are in place.
- There are black bears in Alabama's national forests. Be bear aware.
- You cannot camp near developed recreation areas.
- Campfires are allowed unless there are fire restrictions in effect. Contact the nearest forest service office to be sure.
- Please use existing sites and fire rings.
- Before you leave your campsite, make sure that the campfire is completely out. You should be able to put your whole hand into the ashes without being burned; it should be cool to the touch. Stir the ashes to make sure all embers have cooled. This is very important! Many forest fires are caused by abandoned campfires that were not completely out.
- Use Leave No Trace practices for using the bathroom and washing up.
- There is no safe water source anymore. Water sources have been contaminated so be sure to treat or filter your water before using.

Appendix B: Additional Resources

Alabama's Forever Wild Program
US National Forests in Alabama
2946 Chestnut St., Montgomery, AL 36107
(334) 832-4470
www.fs.usda.gov/detail/alabama/home/?cid=fsbdev3_002552

Alabama State Parks
64 N. Union St., Rm. 538, Montgomery, AL 36130
(800) 252-7275
www.alapark.com

Friends of the Locust Fork
PO Box 638, Cleveland, AL 35049
(205) 274-3537
www.friendsofthelocustforkriver.org

Land Trust of North Alabama
2707 Artie St. SW, Ste. 6, Huntsville, AL 35805
(256) 534-6141
www.landtrustnal.org

The Nature Conservancy
2100 1st Ave. N., Ste. 500, Birmingham, AL 35203
(205) 251-1155
www.nature.org

Sipsey Wilderness Hiking Club
www.sipseywilderness.org

Wild Alabama
552 Lawrence St., Moulton, AL 35650
(256) 974-6166
https://wildal.org

About the Author

Author **Joe Cuhaj** hails from New Jersey but moved to Alabama almost forty years ago and became one of those Yankees—one who fell in love with Alabama's rich biodiversity and landscapes and never went home.

It is here that the former radio broadcaster turned author and freelance writer continued to follow one of his favorite pastimes—hiking and backpacking. In 2000 he combined his love of hiking and writing to pen his first book, *Hike America Alabama*, which was later renamed *Hiking Alabama* and is now in its fifth edition.

Since then, Joe has written four additional outdoor recreation guides for FalconGuides, including *Hiking the Gulf Coast, Hiking through History Alabama, Best Dog Hikes Alabama*, and *Paddling Alabama*, as well as *Best Tent Camping Alabama* for Menasha Ridge Press.

Joe has also penned three historical books—*Space Oddities, Baseball in Mobile*, and *Hidden History of Mobile*—for History Press and has written print articles and web content for several sites and publications on a wide variety of subjects. And falling back into his radio career, he has produced a number of podcasts that can be heard on his website, www.joe-cuhaj.com.

THE TEN ESSENTIALS OF HIKING

American Hiking Society

American Hiking Society recommends you pack the "Ten Essentials" every time you head out for a hike. Whether you plan to be gone for a couple of hours or several months, make sure to pack these items. Become familiar with these items and know how to use them.

1. Appropriate Footwear
Happy feet make for pleasant hiking. Think about traction, support, and protection when selecting well-fitting shoes or boots.

2. Navigation
While phones and GPS units are handy, they aren't always reliable in the backcountry; consider carrying a paper map and compass as a backup and know how to use them.

3. Water (and a way to purify it)
As a guideline, plan for half a liter of water per hour in moderate temperatures/terrain. Carry enough water for your trip and know where and how to treat water while you're out on the trail.

4. Food
Pack calorie-dense foods to help fuel your hike, and carry an extra portion in case you are out longer than expected.

5. Rain Gear & Dry-Fast Layers
The weatherman is not always right. Dress in layers to adjust to changing weather and activity levels. Wear moisture-wicking cloths and carry a warm hat.

6. Safety Items (light, fire, and a whistle)
Have means to start an emergency fire, signal for help, and see the trail and your map in the dark.

7. First Aid Kit

Supplies to treat illness or injury are only as helpful as your knowledge of how to use them. Take a class to gain the skills needed to administer first aid and CPR.

8. Knife or Multi-Tool

With countless uses, a multi-tool can help with gear repair and first aid.

9. Sun Protection

Sunscreen, sunglasses, and sun-protective clothing should be used in every season regardless of temperature or cloud cover.

10. Shelter

Protection from the elements in the event you are injured or stranded is necessary. A lightweight, inexpensive space blanket is a great option.

Find other helpful resources at AmericanHiking.org/hiking-resources

PROTECT THE PLACES YOU LOVE TO HIKE.

Become a member today and take $5 off an annual membership using the code **Falcon5**.

AmericanHiking.org/join

American Hiking Society is the only national nonprofit organization dedicated to empowering all to enjoy, share, and preserve the hiking experience.

American Hiking Society